Pearl & Tim

Here's to

Southern California
in the '50s

...AND YOU...

Charl 3

CHARLES PHOENIX

# Southern CALIFORNIA
## in the '50s

SUN · FUN · FANTASY

ACP
ANGEL CITY PRESS
Santa Monica 2001

ANGEL CITY PRESS

2118 Wilshire Blvd., #880

Santa Monica, California 90403

310.395.9982

www.angelcitypress.com

SOUTHERN CALIFORNIA IN THE '50s : Sun, Fun and Fantasy

by Charles Phoenix

Copyright © 2001 by Charles Phoenix

Design by Kathy Kikkert

FIRST EDITION

10 9 8 7 6 5 4 3 2 1

ISBN 978-1-883318-99-4 (paperbound edition)

LIBRARY OF CONGRESS CATALOGING-IN-PUBLICATION DATA IS AVAILABLE.

Printed in China

# CONTENTS

# Welcome to THE LAND OF PLENTY

Imagine Southern California with two-lane roads meandering through orange groves and oil derricks. Picture suburbs replacing vast expanses of agricultural land. Electric streetcars running on tracks alongside automobiles. McDonald's before

**CONVAIR XF-92A AT EDWARDS AIR FORCE BASE, MOJAVE DESERT, 1952.** Built by the San Diego division of Convair in 1948, it was the world's first delta wing airplane. Its official speed was "high subsonic." During World War II, Southern California produced more aircraft than any other state in the country. These industries were the economic backbone of many other communities including Long Beach, Pomona, Lakewood, Santa Monica and Inglewood, where major manufacturing facilities were located. The hub of the aircraft and aerospace industry was El Segundo, conveniently located adjacent to Los Angeles International Airport.

**OIL DERRICKS, LOS ANGELES, 1955.** Southern California's first oil boom of 1892 was followed by another in the '20s when California's most productive oil fields were discovered in Torrance, Inglewood, Santa Fe Springs, Huntington Beach and Signal Hill in Long Beach. In 1936, the oil field of Wilmington was discovered and became the state's biggest all-time producer. By the '50s, Southern California's industries, cars and utilities had grown to the point where they absorbed much of the state's output of gasoline, diesel and fuel oils. Throughout the decade, the search for more oil in the area continued both on land and beneath the sea. In 1951 a man-made drilling island was constructed just off the coast at Seal Beach. By 1955, fifty-five wells were producing from the island.

it served billions. Drive-in theaters in every community. Freeways emerging and merging. Disneyland opening its magical doors to a kingdom of make-believe for the very first time. This was Southern California in the 1950s.

Eons ago Mother Nature blessed Southern California with a more than generous serving of her finest fair weather, fertile valleys, sunny shores and snow-capped mountain peaks. Native Americans were the first documented civilization to call the enchanted land home. In the mid-1500s, Spanish explorers found their way to an inlet that would one day be the port of San Diego and things would never be the same. In 1769, threatened by other European explorers, the Spaniards claimed the land they called Alta California as their own and began building landmark missions.

Beginning in 1784, enormous land grants were awarded to several Spanish Army veterans who established their own ranchos as places to retire and raise herds of cattle.

By 1781, when the pueblo of Los Angeles was established as the social and trading center for the rancheros, San Diego and Santa Barbara were already lively little villages. Forty years later, when Mexico gained its independence from Spain, Mexican settlers began coming to Los Angeles and helped establish the little village as an active market for cattle hides and fat, which were to be traded with the United States. In 1848, Mexican rule ended in California; two years later the territory became a state and Los Angeles, with a population of slightly more than sixteen hundred, was incorporated as a city. During the ensuing decade, Southern California ranchers became wealthy by supplying cattle to the thousands of prospectors who had flocked to Northern California during

the Gold Rush that had begun in 1849. Later, in the 1860s, the ranchos were subdivided and much of the land was sold to wealthy land barons from all over the United States. Increasing numbers of pioneers traveled west in covered wagons to begin a new life ranching and farming, ultimately setting the stage for the rise of Southern California as a population center.

When the Southern Pacific Railroad reached Los Angeles in 1876, the seaside towns of San Diego, Santa Barbara, Santa Monica, Wilmington, Ventura and Long Beach and the inland communities of Santa Ana, Pasadena and San Bernardino were bustling with activity. The thriving local economy was based on sales of cattle, fruit and wheat. By the early 1880s, people were coming in droves to the fertile lands of Southern California. All were seeking the health, prosperity and happiness promised by the promotional literature of the day, propaganda that claimed that Southern California was, among other things, "the land of sunshine, subdivisions and perpetual spring," where a family could live well on ten acres and a farmer could live the life of "a country gentleman." One of the colorful railroad posters that hung in stations across the country read: "California . . . the cornucopia of the World . . . room for millions of immigrants . . . railroad and private land for a

million farmers . . . a climate for health and wealth with no cyclones or blizzards."

Just after the Santa Fe Railroad completed its line to Los Angeles in 1885, the California Excursion Association was organized to turn the attention of the United States to Southern California. The railroads had land to sell and they had great interest in moving people west. A raging rate war between the railroads brought the price of a ticket from Kansas City to Los Angeles to only a dollar—albeit for only one day in 1887— and migration reached record numbers.

Large and small plots of land were selling as fast as they could be subdivided; real estate prices peaked. Civic boosters and real estate salesmen attracted crowds of potential buyers with bands, elephants, free lunches and freak shows. New towns such as Glendale, Burbank, Monrovia, Arcadia, Claremont, Pomona, Ontario, Redlands, La Jolla, Orange, Santa Ana, Fullerton and Whittier were established. By the late 1880s, with bountiful crops of citrus, walnuts, grapes and olives, agriculture

WATTS TOWERS, LOS ANGELES, 1959. A masterpiece of folk art, the Watts Towers were created by Italian immigrant Simon Rodia. Working alone, he built his towers as a tribute to his adopted country and a monument to the spirit of individuals who had made their dream a reality. Constructed between 1921 and 1954 in the small triangle-shaped yard next to his house in South Central Los Angeles, the towers were handmade without any machine equipment, scaffolding, bolts, rivets, or welds. Using simple hand tools, Rodia shaped scrap steel pipes wrapped in wire mesh, then coated them with mortar and embellished them with colorful broken bits and pieces of glass, ceramic tiles, bottlecaps and seashells. In the 1940s, Rodia was asked by city inspectors about the height of his three tallest towers. He replied that he built them in honor of the California Highways 101, 99 and Route 66, so they were 101, 99 and 66 feet tall. By the time he finished working on the towers in 1954, they had been discovered as one of Los Angeles's most unusual tourist attractions. In 1957, city officials declared the towers unsafe and tried to tear them down. But when the wrecking ball hit the towers, it failed, and the towers proved sturdy enough to survive.

became the new base of the economy. Elaborate seaside resort towns such as Venice, Redondo Beach and Long Beach drew people to the shores. In 1892, oil was discovered in Los Angeles and Southern California was on its way to becoming an industrial, as well as agricultural, giant.

Between 1900 and 1920, the regional population quadrupled to well over one million. With the completion of the California Aqueduct in 1913, there was a seemingly endless water supply for large-scale urban growth. By the 1920s the Pacific Electric Railway's network of "Red Car" trolleys based in Los Angeles was the most extensive metropolitan mass transit system in the world. Los Angeles had surpassed San Francisco as California's largest city and manufacturing center, and had more cars on the road than any other city in the country.

Southern Californians discovered their love affair with not only the automobile but with the airplane as well. The first international air meet in the Western Hemisphere was held on the outskirts of Los Angeles in 1910. A budding aircraft industry was born from the talents of local entrepreneurs like Donald Douglas and the Lockheed brothers. By 1922 the Douglas plant in Santa Monica was turning out an airplane a week.

While Hollywood became the movie capital of the world it also became the world's greatest publicity machine. Hollywood exposed Southern California as a very progressive, playful and trendy society. With the help of the film industry's army of creative types, it gave a designer touch to everything from homes to restaurants to cars. Southern California was developing its own "look." Helping to spread the word was press hungry for any news of Hollywood. When Los Angeles hosted the Olympic Games in 1932, Southern California received worldwide publicity and became known

CHAMBER OF COMMERCE BROCHURE, RIVERSIDE, 1952. Typical of the promotional brochures of the era listing facts and figures about population, housing, etc., this brochure tends to glamorize and glorify things a bit by claiming, among other things: "Riverside's industries are nuisance free with no pollution of air, water or soil."

DRIFTWOOD DAIRY BILLBOARD, EL MONTE, 1953. By the '50s, cattle ranching and dairy farming had long been a mainstay of the local economy. Hundreds of dairies developed in the rural communities surrounding Los Angeles. The cities of Artesia, Norwalk and Cerritos were known as Dairyland. In the late '50s when tract-home developments replaced dairy pastures, many dairy farmers moved their cows and dairy facilities to Chino.

*Sunset Brand orange crate label, early 1950s.*
Long before the '50s, Southern California was as famous for its orange groves as it was for its Hollywood stars. The fragrant citrus groves that blanketed major portions of the valleys across Riverside, San Bernardino, Orange, Los Angeles and Ventura counties, produced more than half the citrus grown in the United States. In 1950, the citrus packing houses in Corona and Ontario were the world's largest. But, in the next ten years, thousands of acres of Southern California's orange groves were bulldozed to make way subdivisions of tract homes, schools, supermarkets, shopping centers, industry and other developments, including Disneyland.

as the land of the rich, famous, healthy and beautiful people.

Los Angeles County became the fifth-largest industrial complex in the United States. By 1938, a network of revolutionary superhighways was on the drawing boards of engineers and urban planners. Two years later, the Arroyo Seco Parkway (now called the Pasadena Freeway) opened, linking downtown Los Angeles with Pasadena; Southern California's first freeway was complete. During World War II, Southern California defined what President Dwight Eisenhower later called the "American military-industrial complex," and its economy, population and employment opportunities

continued to soar. The federal government built large military bases in the region and invested billions of dollars in the local aircraft and aerospace industries, shipyards and war-related manufacturing plants. Southern California emerged from the war as a superpower. Hundreds of thousands of servicemen returning from overseas, the wartime workers and their families found it the perfect place to settle and begin a new life. Construction, manufacturing and productivity was at a fever pitch. Success bred success, expansion knew no bounds. Southern California was ready for a prosperous new decade.

In the '50s, Southern California was

indeed the place to be. The mood was up, prosperity ruled and the deluxe standard of space-age living was flying high. It was the promised land for a new generation of movers and shakers who reinvented the standard of living and created a cultural explosion of American pie. It was the perfect indoor-outdoor combination of town and country, work and play.

*Welcome to Southern California in the '50s . . . Sun, Fun and Fantasy!*

VERNON'S California Casual

**CALIFORNIA POTTERY, 1954.** "California Casual" by Vernon sported "magnificent colors in the modern mood." A sixteen-piece service for four was $7.95. Pottery production began in Southern California in the early 1900s. By the '40s the colorful dishes and decorative pieces from local manufacturers such as Metlox, Vernon and Bauer were a common sight in kitchens and dining rooms throughout the Unites States. Due to restrictions on imports during World War II, the pottery business flourished and by 1950 there were more than eight hundred pottery manufacturers in Southern California. After the war, when import restrictions were lifted, imports from Japan and Italy flooded the market. By the late '50s many pottery factories were unable to compete with the lower-cost imports and shut their doors.

**ARTS AND ARCHITECTURE MAGAZINE COVER, MAY 1952.** Published in Los Angeles, *Arts and Architecture* was a progressive magazine that showcased the work of innovative modern architects, designers and manufacturers. In 1945, just after the war ended, the editor, John Entenza, created and sponsored one of Southern California's most significant contributions to modern architecture, the Case Study House program. It was conceived to promote innovative and sophisticated modern "form-follows-function" architectural styles and the use of affordable new building materials and techniques for the postwar housing boom. Between 1946 and 1962, twenty-eight experimental modern single-family prototype homes were built in the Los Angeles area. They were designed by Southern California's leading modernists including Richard Neutra, Pierre Koenig, Craig Ellwood and Charles Eames, architects and designers whose names would become legendary. Ultimately the program influenced a generation of architects working for mostly wealthy clients building custom modern homes.

arts & architecture

MAY 1952

5

## Heavenly Bodies

### the "Wing Ding"

Cole's soaring new silhouette —
a one-piece shorts swimsuit — to
embrace you in heavenly form. Wear
the winged bra up or down (for adding
or subtracting). Couturier detailed inside
and out by Cole designer Margit Fellegi . . .
in richly corded Lastex rimmed with
nylon laton. *22.95 at fine stores.*

**Cole**
OF CALIFORNIA
ORIGINAL

Cole of California ad, 1952. During the '50s, Southern California was the world's second-largest clothing manufacturing center, and apparel was the state's fifth-largest industry. Specializing in swimwear and casual sportswear, a "made in California" label from a Southern California designer or manufacturer became a status symbol in better department stores and shops across the United States.

# Chapter 1

# ON THE MOVE

Southern California had become the car capital of the world by 1950. The colorful car culture enveloped every part of daily life. The car inspired adventure, provided unprecedented independence and influenced everything from the layout of new housing developments to the form and function of new signs and new buildings. Mobility with style, speed, status and convenience were top priorities. Cars became the ultimate "grand prize," the trophies that owners treasured, pampered, raced, displayed, customized and catered to. With the expansion of the freeway system, cars took us from the past and into the future and forever changed the landscape, lifestyle and route between city and suburbia.

In 1949, construction began on the "stack," the crown jewel four-level freeway interchange in downtown Los Angeles. Southern California's freeway system had begun on the drawing boards in the '30s and by 1940, the first section, the Pasadena Freeway, was complete. After World War II, construction began on the San Bernardino and Santa Ana Freeways. The "stack" linked them all. Throughout the '50s, freeway construction continued stretch by stretch at a rapid pace. As each section was completed, it was celebrated with a ribbon cutting and "first ride" ceremony.

More and faster roads translated to a lifestyle on the move. Southern California's booming trailer and mobile home industry came of age in 1954 when the first annual "Trailer Life Show" was held in Los Angeles at the Shrine Exposition Hall. Billing it as "the greatest trailer show in the world," local manufacturers including Silver Streak, Airfloat, Road Master and Airstream, who were together producing more than 250,000 units a year, displayed their latest and most luxurious models. The Pan American Trailer Coach Co. of Monrovia unveiled its new "Panoramic" model. According to the deluxe brochure, "There has never been any-

BUILT BY THE WORLD'S LARGEST BUILDERS OF MOBILE HOMES
The PAN-AMERICAN "Panoramic" for '54
PALATIAL ..... LUXURIOUS ..... INSPIRED!
PANORAMIC BAY WINDOW
PANORAMIC SLIDING GLASS DOOR
SUPERLATIVE

thing like the palatial 'Panoramic' before. Mere words cannot fully describe the utter beauty and the actual splendor of this magnificent inspiration of engineering genius. It's a millionaire's dream come true."

Since General Motors, Ford and Chrysler all had huge auto assembly plants operating in Southern California, a local cult of after-hours backyard and garage mechanics and body men were building their own cars, hot rods and custom models. Most hot rods were modified Ford Model T or Model A roadsters. They were cheap and plentiful in local junkyards. Standard procedure was to strip off the fenders, running boards and trim, to achieve maximum weight reduction and aerodynamics. Ford flathead V8 engines were the power plants of choice. Custom cars were created for their appearance and not for their performance. The vehicles' rooflines were chopped and frames were lowered. Fenders, grilles, taillights and other parts from two or three different makes of cars were mixed and matched together for extraordinary effect. No expense was spared on fancy pinstriping, flames and "Kandy Kolored" metallic paint. Ultimately Southern California's hot rod and custom car builders influenced the golden age of Detroit's flamboyant fins and the Easter egg colors of the late '50s and the high performance muscle cars of the '60s.

Encouraged by the fact that most families had two cars in the '50s so that stay-at-home women could more efficiently run their households, businesses such as dairies, dry cleaners, banks, donut shops and burger stands began offering the ultimate convenience: drive-through service. The concept of drive-through was a simple leap from the idea of the drive-in restaurant (with barbecue-beef sandwiches, fried chicken and hamburgers on the menu) that had evolved shortly after the first drive-through gas stations appeared in the '20s. In 1948, people who ordered food from their car were still accustomed to being served by carhops and eating their car fare with knives and forks. That's when Southern California's first drive-through hamburger stand, In 'n' Out Burger started in Baldwin Park, pioneering the idea of ordering only burgers, fries and drinks from a two-way speaker. That same year in San Bernardino, the McDonald brothers, successful but tired of running a traditional drive-in restaurant, eliminated carhops, limited the menu to hamburgers, French fries and milk shakes, and introduced the "Speedee service system" from walk-up windows and revolutionized the food-service business.

Balmy nights made drive-in theaters a natural in Southern California, so the first outdoor cinema opened in West Los Angeles in 1934. After World War II, the drive-in theater construction boom began. Enormous painted murals like the flamenco dancers at the El Monte, and the Viking ships at the Compton Drive-in decorated many of the screen towers. Many drive-ins had pre-show picnic tables and kiddie playgrounds. By 1950,

Pacific Drive-in Theaters, the largest local chain, had fourteen locations. Pacific promoted its theaters as family entertainment and advertised "no sitter problems, free bottle warming, children under 12 free, color cartoons nightly, large clean restrooms, modern snack bars, smoke if you'd like, and invalids love it." With the increase of cars among families and teenagers, the popularity of drive-in theaters skyrocketed. The combination of cars and movies under the stars inspired drive-in theater names such as the Big Sky in Duarte, the Sundown in Whittier and the Starlite in El Monte.

As drive-ins began getting a reputation as teenage passion pits, some drive-in theaters started holding Sunday morning drive-in church services to help preserve a moral balance. By 1955, Reverend Robert Schuller began preaching the gospel from the tarpaper roof of the snack bar at the Orange Drive-in in the city of Orange, county of Orange. More congregations on wheels developed, spurred on by slogans such as "Worship as you are in the family car" and "Honk to say amen." It was fitting that the automobile had helped Southern California find religion.

PANORAMIC TRAILER, MONROVIA, 1954. This forty-five-foot mobile mansion, designed and built in Southern California, featured a bay window and sliding glass door. With freeways making destinations easier to reach and homes on wheels in great supply, driving vacations became family fare. The term "recreational vehicle" hadn't been coined yet, but '50s vacation trailers were the beginning of the camper craze that would sweep the country.

MOBIL TRAILER ESTATES, SAN BERNARDINO, 1958. Trailer parks were popular in beach, desert and suburban communities. Typically they were in a garden or orange-grove setting. The most deluxe parks featured a shuffleboard court, clubhouse and swimming pool, and had names such as Shady Grove, Desert Dunes, Treasure Isle or Ponderosa Pines. Many of the residents were seasonal visitors.

MINIATURE TRAIN, TRAVEL TOWN, GRIFFITH PARK, LOS ANGELES, 1953. Dedicated in 1952, Travel Town, a "hands on" railroad museum, was the idea of local railroad enthusiasts who thought a steam locomotive would make an interesting attraction next to the miniature railroad in Griffith Park. About that time the steam locomotive era was ending and the major California railroads were contacted and asked to donate their old trains that were destined for the scrap yard. By the late '50s, Travel Town was one of the west's largest collections of retired locomotives, trolleys and streetcars.

"THE LONG BEACH LIMITED," 1958. The Limited, which traveled between Los Angeles and Long Beach, was one of the last operating Pacific Electric Red Cars. Beginning in 1901, the Red Cars, a network of streetcars, connected Los Angeles, Orange, San Bernardino and Riverside counties. Powered by overhead electrical cables, the streetcars shared the boulevards and avenues, running right alongside cars and trucks. By 1920, at its peak, with nine hundred cars and eleven hundred miles of track, the system was Southern California's primary mode of transportation and the world's largest interurban trolley system. Over the next few decades, the Red Cars slowly fell victim to Angelenos' love of automobiles. Gas rationing during World War II temporarily preserved ridership, which reached its peak in 1944. By 1950, cars had taken over the roads. Gasoline, tire, insurance and automobile interests helped make certain that the legendary line would be shut down. During the '50s, Red Car devotees mourned the continual succession of "last runs." By 1959, only one line, from Los Angeles to Long Beach, remained in operation. After sixty years of faithful service, the last Red Car ran on this line in 1961.

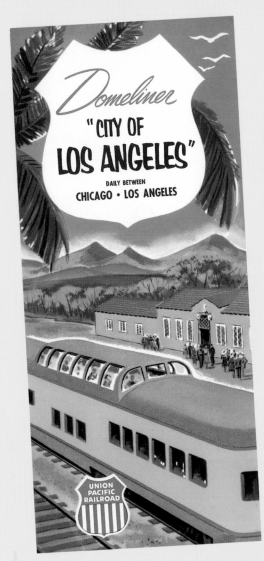

A monumental feat of engineering, the new state-of-the-art highway system made it convenient for Southern Californians to work downtown and live in the suburbs.

## The Freeway System

UNION PACIFIC RAILROAD "CITY OF LOS ANGELES" BROCHURE, 1958. In the '50s, for those who wished to travel in or out of town the old-fashioned way, Southern Pacific, Union Pacific and Sante Fe Railroads served Southern California. To compete with the soaring popularity of air and auto travel, they offered new bubble-topped observation cars called Domeliners. Union Pacific's "City of Los Angeles" train had three novelty cars, the dome coach, dome lounge car and dome diner.

The four-level interchange, completed in 1953, was the first highway high-rise, the new heart of town and prototype for the future of auto transportation.

19

The first Big Donut Drive-in, at the corner of Century Boulevard and Normandie Avenue, Los Angeles, 1955. Opened in 1954, there were five locations: the original, Inglewood, Gardena, Culver City and Compton. It later became Randy's Donuts. Few photographs exist of the early Big Donut days.

SUPREME FARMS DRIVE-IN DAIRY, PASADENA, 1954.
Suburban communities began developing close to once-rural dairy farms. Farmers capitalized on the increase in passing traffic by building drive-in dairies at the edge of their pastures.

**MCDONALD'S HAMBURGERS, ALHAMBRA, 1954.** Before franchising their business in 1952, the enterprising McDonald brothers hired Fontana architect Stanley Meston to design an eye-catching "trademark" building to house their new streamlined burger-and-fries operation. With Speedee as their mascot and crowned by what would become world-renowned golden arches, the result was inviting with a stylish wedge-shaped roof, gleaming red-and-white tile and plenty of diagonal glass— all designed to showcase the innovative food-preparation and service system.

Nixon's Drive-in, Whittier, 1954. Owned and operated by President Nixon's brother Donald in their hometown, Nixon's Drive-in opened in 1952. One of the most popular spots for cruising teens, Nixon's offered convenient walk-up or drive-through service, "The modern self-service way of dining out with the family," it was advertised as "truly Californian and surrounded by a grove of orange trees." The menu included country fried chicken, fried shrimp, fish and chips, salads, steak sandwiches, homemade pies, fresh-squeezed orange juice, malts, milkshakes and the double-decker Nixon Burger with cheese, of course.

Harvey's Broiler, 1961. During the '50s there were countless drive-in restaurants with carhop service in Southern California. Harvey's Broiler, opened in 1958 in Downey, was one of the last and largest ever built.

Drive-ins & Drive-throughs

Bob's Big Boy, Toluca Lake, 1952. In the '50s, cruising the boulevard and going back and forth between local drive-in restaurants were popular weekend evening activities for teenagers. They socialized and showed off their cars. After the heyday of Southern California's drive-in restaurants in the '30s and '40s, by the early '50s, these younger patrons began to be a serious problem. They ordered very little, took up parking spaces for hours and tended to be a rowdy bunch. But worse was that the adult and family crowds stayed away from what they regarded as teen hangouts. Many establishments discontinued carhop service in an attempt to bring back families.

**VALLEY DRIVE-IN THEATER, BETWEEN POMONA AND ONTARIO ON HIGHWAY 99.** Built in 1948, the world's largest neon mural made this Southern California's most spectacular drive-in. Originally surrounded by orange groves, this deluxe drive-in covered almost thirty acres, accommodated eight hundred cars and offered two hundred outdoor seats for walk-in customers. The eight-story screen tower, painted forest green, framed the giant four-thousand-square-foot hand-painted mural of the Santa Barbara mission. Outlined with almost a half-mile of neon, the mural had animated oxcart wheels, a priest with a blue neon Bible and "flowing" light that moved to represent a stream. In 1949, in a novel attempt to amuse moviegoers before the show started, "Monkeyland," a miniature monkey zoo advertised as "another drive-in first," opened alongside the children's playground. In 1954, when the screen was widened and curved to fit Cinemascope films, it was the largest outdoor screen in the United States.

**CAR CLUB OF THE YEAR**

# CAR CRAFT

**FEBRUARY 1959**
**25c**

**THE SECRET'S OUT!**

**"CANDY" COLORS**

Materials Needed
Mixing Formulas
How To Apply

WILD CHERRY
PAGAN GOLD    PEARL
ORIENTAL BLUE
MINT GREEN    LIME GOLD
CANDY RED

see page 18

**FEBRUARY 1955 ISSUE OF *CAR CRAFT* MAGAZINE.** One of the many hot rod and custom car magazines that began publication in Los Angeles in the early '50s, it featured the cars, "how-tos," car shows, drag races and usually some cheesecake. The cover story of this issue featured the king of the car customizers, George Barris of Barris's Kustom Kars Shop in Lynwood.

The "Golden Sahara," one of George Barris's most spectacular custom cars posing with a Chris Craft powerboat at the Salton Sea, 1958.

**SAN FERNANDO DRAG STRIP, 1959.** In 1951, the National Hot Rod Association was founded in Los Angeles. The goal was to change the image of hot rodding as the pastime of juvenile delinquents and teenage gangs, promote cooperation between hot rodders and police and to create drag strips to replace impromptu street racing.

25

# Chapter 2

# SUBURBIA

Tract homes. Shopping centers. Swimming pools. Patios. Barbecues. Parks and playgrounds. These were the visual components of suburbia, Southern California style, circa 1950. The suburbs were the place to live, shop and play, all in a spacious,

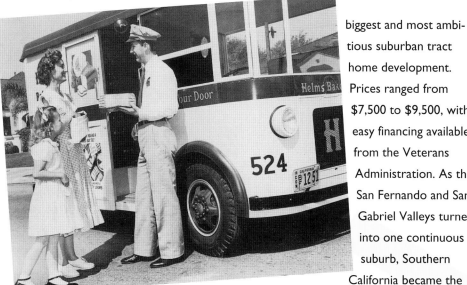

auto-friendly, landscaped garden setting planned for gracious and carefree family living. The lifestyle that had been merely a dream to the last generation, became a reality for its children.

As the population continued to explode and cities and towns overflowed, enterprising builders, developers and speculators quickly subdivided and transformed vast expanses of fragrant orange groves, rural ranches, bean fields and dairy farms into instant communities with all the trimmings. Lakewood, a new town just north of Long Beach, was promoted as the "city of tomorrow." The "future was unlimited" in Downey, and Glendora was "the land of exotic living."

Tract homes were designed to be built at low cost on a mass scale and the demand required a frantic construction pace. The city of Lakewood was the biggest and most ambitious suburban tract home development. Prices ranged from $7,500 to $9,500, with easy financing available from the Veterans Administration. As the San Fernando and San Gabriel Valleys turned into one continuous suburb, Southern California became the tract house capital of the world. Each subdivision or tract was labeled and advertised with a name such as Highland Glen in La Mirada or Flamingo Rancho in Whittier. Buyers were sold "custom-built quality, lasting value and endless pride of ownership." Housewives, a plentiful breed in the 1950s, were enticed by architectural details they thought would remain contemporary throughout a lifetime, as well as the convenience and timesaving features of the latest built-in appliances.

While most tracts offered variations of traditional, modern or ranch architectural styles, some combined and created hybrid combinations of two or all three. By far, however, the majority of new buyers preferred ranch-style homes. Custom home builders sometimes took the ranch style and crossed it with oriental details to create a pagoda-ranch look. Model homes were often furnished a la the "Disneyland" school, with early American living rooms, space-age kitchens and tropical patios.

New tract and custom homes perfected and epitomized what the press promoted as "California style." Designed for new more informal indoor-outdoor living, the houses featured sliding glass doors and the open single-story floor plan and patio of classic California ranch houses. Patios were reinvented as outdoor "rooms" and became the place at home to relax and entertain. Outdoor furnishings and appointments were often given as much consideration as those inside the home. Portable barbecues were essential and backyard swimming pools were suburbia's ultimate status symbol.

Along with the spread of suburban tract homes came a new generation of garden apartment buildings. These two-story stucco boxes offered a sampler of the popular housing styles of the day. Seeing three or more apartment buildings on a block sitting side by side was common, all with different façade motifs. Some were dressed in stylized traditional trim, while others wore ranch, Polynesian and other themed façades. Fashionable names, such as Aloha Gardens, Pool and Patio and Flamingo Capri, generously spelled out in a stylish font, labeled the front of each building.

Decorative futuristic back-lit starburst and disc fixtures provided dramatic night lighting. A sparkling swimming pool was the centerpiece of most courtyards, and landscaping was always lush.

Homeowners and apartment dwellers alike appreciated the luxuries, necessities and services that were more than plentiful in the suburbs. Modern shopping centers, department stores, strip malls and supermarkets became the focal points of new developments. Supermarket grand openings were often the suburbs' biggest spectacles. Alpha Beta and Ralphs were among the first chains in Southern California to establish full-scale supermarkets. While many older, smaller markets were remodeled and remained in operation, Ralphs, Alpha Beta and other

local grocery chains such as Vons, Safeway, Shopping Bag, and Market Basket rapidly began expanding and building larger supermarkets in new suburban developments. These stores were promoted as ultra-luxurious with automatic doors, window walls and air conditioning.

The bigger, more deluxe retail developments such as Lakewood Center, Fashion Square in Santa Ana and Eastland in West Covina had a single major department store to "anchor" them (that is, to pull in a steady clientele) and a decided designer touch. Specialty stores lined stylish outdoor promenades and courtyards, separated physically and visually from the lots where cars were parked. The shopping havens were landscaped with tropical greenery in raised planters with built-in seating areas. Fountains, modern garden art and piped in Muzak, completed the utopian effect. These new suburban shopping centers quickly replaced Southern California's vintage Main Street shopping districts and reinvented retail merchandising.

1950s Alpha Beta matchbook, "where Southern California saves."

HELMS BAKERY AD, 1950. Begun in 1931, The Helms Bakery was based in West Los Angeles. Throughout the '50s, its distinct "toot-toot" whistles would signal that the Helmsman had arrived in the neighborhood. This scene was repeated on a daily basis all over Southern California by a fleet of approximately five hundred butter-colored coaches. Children would race to the Helms truck and their moms would follow to buy fresh bread, cakes cookies, donuts and brownies artfully displayed in long pull-out wooden drawers. The Helmsman wore an official Helms hat, a bow tie and a shiny chrome coin changer on his belt.

BACKYARD BARBECUE, WITH SCHLITZ BEER IN HAND, BELLFLOWER, 1954. No suburban patio or backyard was complete without a barbecue. Cooking outdoors over an open flame brought out the suburban caveman.

**"X" RANCH TRACT HOMES, ANAHEIM, 1957.** For these homes, located three blocks west of Disneyland, a ranch mink stole was the top prize in a promotional "name the tract" contest, and mink scarves were awarded for the three winning names of each of the five different models. Ranch Homes were the gingerbread houses of suburbia. They were characterized by their decorative wood-work trim, windows with diamond panes and shutters, used-brick chimneys, mock rooftop birdhouses, shake roofs and garage doors detailed like faux barn doors. Some builders took the theme to an extreme and fashioned garages in the shape of barns.

## Ranch Style

**FARM HOUSE WINDMILL, RESTAURANT SIGN, 1958.** Lit with two thousand feet of neon, spinning and towering sixty feet, this landmark windmill sign was erected in 1958 to attract passing motorists on the new Santa Ana Freeway to the Farm House and the Buttery, two ranch-style restaurants in Buena Park.

**THE FARM HOUSE MOTEL, RIVERSIDE, 1958.** Alongside the spread of ranch-style homes in suburbia, many shops, dinner houses, apart-ments, motels, office buildings and markets were also finished with a ranch-style motif. This motel has a barn-shaped neon sign, drinking trough as a planter and fiberglass horse pulling an antique buggy.

HAPPY MOTHERS MAKE HAPPY HOMES

In Flamingo Rancho mother can finally enjoy some of the casual California living everybody writes about and talks about—but which Kenbo Corporation has actually done something about! Scientific room arrangement, planned with her preferences specifically in mind, will make mother happy as a lark. So will Flamingo Rancho's labor-saving Blue Flame kitchen!

KENBO
CORPORATION

FLAMINGO
Rancho

WHITTIER · CALIFORNIA

Postcard advertising four model tract homes, Glendora, 1955. Many new tracts featured economical and much less embellished versions of the ranch-style home. The clean lines and rock roof led builders to advertise this as "modern."

"Flamingo Rancho" brochure, Whittier, 1956. "Whittier has become the favored residential city for the busy executive and professional man. Here he can raise his family in an atmosphere of culture and dignity," says this tract-home brochure.

Chamber of Commerce brochure cover, Downey, 1958. "Gracious living . . . future unlimited." This is a typical upscale custom-built suburban ranch home with tropical patio and swimming pool. During the '50s, Anthony Bros. was Southern California's leading pool builder. The business began in 1947 when cement contractor Phil Anthony, built a pool for his family at their Pasadena home. When friends and neighbors saw his aquatic creation they wanted one just like it. At the time, there were just five swimming pool builders in Southern California. By 1959, when Anthony Bros. Swimming Pools was headquartered on fifteen acres in South Gate and had eighteen local regional offices, there were more than one hundred local pool builders.

Backyard pool party group photo, Los Angeles, 1957.

Gracious living . . . future unlimited . . . Downey

COMPLIMENTARY
DOWNEY CHAMBER OF COMMERCE
COPY

Pools & Patios

**BIRD'S EYE VIEW OF "THE CITY OF TOMORROW," LAKEWOOD, 1952.** Covering more than ten square miles, the city of Lakewood was the world's largest planned community. Since each house was equipped with a Waste King Pulverator, it was also called the "world's first garbage-free city." Started from scratch in 1950, by 1953 Lakewood had 135 miles of freshly paved streets, twenty parks, ten new schools and seventeen thousand cookie cutter homes, all surrounding a shopping center. Construction was begun on fifty or more homes each day, so houses were built in record time, assembly-line style. The houses sold as fast as the workers could build them. As each subdivision was completed, buyers lined up. One Saturday, a hundred houses were sold in one hour.

**HORACE HEIDT'S MAGNOLIA ESTATE APARTMENTS, SHERMAN OAKS, DESIGNER RENDERING, 1957.** Between 1955 and 1962, famed big band leader Horace Heidt transformed his Sherman Oaks orange ranch into an enormous garden apartment complex, a home for his troupe of entertainers when they weren't on the road. His original 1939 ranch house was left intact and became the office. With an imaginary center dividing line, he themed the lush indoor-outdoor living quarters after his two favorite resort destinations, Palm Springs and Hawaii. Just inside beyond the lilac-covered drive-through entrance were two spectacular rock waterfalls. On the Palm Springs side the waterfall had dyed blue water and, on the Hawaii side, red water to create the feeling of an erupting

volcano. The whimsical resort motif was repeated throughout the grounds with a tiki-hut-style guard shack, hand-carved gnarly wood directional signs, dancing water fountains and an aviary with exotic birds. The complex included four swimming pools, tennis and shuffleboard courts and a clubhouse where entertainment was never in short supply. The most unusual feature was a miniature nineteen-hole golf course recreating the most famous holes from the world's most famous golf courses.

**FIVE GUYS TAKE A BREAK ON MOVE-IN DAY, INGLEWOOD, 1958.** Typical of a street of '50s apartments, one building has a modern façade and the one right next door is ranch style. These mix-and-match façades were often constructed by the same builder and went up at the same time. The apartments typically had identical floor plans and minimal interior detail.

**MR. PEANUT AT RALPHS GRAND OPENING, ENCINO, 1952.** By the '50s, Ralphs was Southern California's oldest and largest supermarket chain. Its publicity department made certain that every grand opening, anniversary and store remodeling made the local newspaper. Many grand openings were broadcast live on local television and were often commentated by popular local television personalities. During the '50s, the three-day promotional celebrations included kiddie rides, clowns, monkey and circus acts, country western bands, beauty contests, free buffets, giant cakes in the shape of the new market and fashion shows on runways built over the frozen food display cases. There were contests with prizes that included free groceries, deep fryers, appliances, lawnmowers, radios, sewing machines, travel trailers, cars and all-expense-paid vacations to Acapulco, as well as bicycles, red wagons, dolls and Davy Crockett hats for the kids. The next day, local newspaper headlines would detail the excitement: "Thrills Galore During Ralphs Grand Opening" and "Fashions Flower Amidst Frozen Food."

**OXNARD SHOPPING CENTER, 1959.** Typical of Southern California's most common neighborhood suburban shopping centers, this retail development had a supermarket as its anchor store, with a pharmacy, five-and-ten, dress shop, shoe store, bakery, beauty salon, barber shop and other necessity stores. The style of these neighborhood shopping centers was no-nonsense, form-follows-function, with flat façades that served as large backgrounds for colorful neon signs.

*Supermarkets & Strip Malls*

## Shopping Centers

*Eastland Shopping Center, West Covina, 1957.* Built bordering a newly completed stretch of the San Bernardino Freeway, Eastland was the first shopping center in Southern California to be freeway friendly. The spectacular stained-glass sign tower was visible from miles away. Like the Lakewood Center, there were no loading docks for any of the stores at ground level. A half-mile-long tunnel connected the basements of the stores to keep delivery trucks out of sight. These tunnels were also marked Civil Defense fallout shelters. They each had enough room to hold thousands in the event of nuclear attack.

**MAY CO., LAKEWOOD CENTER, 1952.** *The* centerpiece of the "world's largest tract home development," and the tallest building in town, May Co. was the anchor of Lakewood Center. The giant yellow neon M's that marked the building on four sides were each nineteen feet tall and visible from every street in town. The department store was stocked with everything it took to make a home.

*Employee group photo in front of Sears, Valley Plaza, North Hollywood, 1955.*
Beginning in the '30s, Sears was one of the first department store chains in Southern California to revolutionize retailing by building large suburban stores away from crowded downtowns. During the '50s, the retail giant built many local suburban stores. As if bearing a title on a giant movie screen, each store carried the neon-lined "Sears" in green-enameled script.

*Lakewood Shopping Center, designer rendering, 1952.* The utopian-style pedestrian promenade and shops of Lakewood Center were to be literally the center of town. More than just a shopping center, with office buildings, restaurants, a bowling center, theater, post office and the civic center, Lakewood Center was the modern equivalent of the classic town square. There were 12,000 parking spaces.

Chapter 3

# SPACE-AGE STYLE

In the '50s Southern California was out of this world. The sky was the limit and the look of tomorrow was the latest. Because the area was the center of the universe when it came to aircraft and aerospace development and manufacturing, the idea of applying space-age lingo and shapes to the visual landscape was the local trend. While kids in school were being taught to "duck and cover" in school and while Dad was building a bomb shelter in the backyard, a flying saucer (albeit man-made on this planet) was about to land at Los Angeles International Airport and another at the Elks Lodge in Long Beach. Rocket ships, neon signs, coffee shops, churches, bowling alleys, even "Drifty" the cow and the local bakery's bread were all poised for takeoff . . . destination moon! Tomorrowland at Disneyland Park was a prototype for "the world of 1987." And new apartment buildings and everyday businesses—dry cleaners, motels, cocktail lounges and muffler shops—had galactic names like Galaxy, Orbit, Rocket, Saturn, Satellite and Jet-Age.

From the drawing boards to the factories to the runways and launch pads, the transition

from the jet age to the space age had arrived. In the decade before the first scheduled passenger jet departed from Los Angeles International Airport in 1959, new materials, building technology, construction techniques and stylized visions of the future were in great supply. For a generation of local artists, designers and architects, it was an opportunity to experiment and reinvent the shapes and styles of signs, buildings and environments. To builders, developers and businessmen, the time was right to sell the future. And for Southern Californians, it was a chance to "live" the future. From the chic and sophisticated to the nifty and the novel, a whole new set of design standards and details broke, or at least bent, all the rules. The form-follows-function rule of design took on new meaning: the form was aerodynamically eye-catching and the function reassured the customer that the future was now.

In architecture, the post and beam were taken to the extreme. Rooflines slanted skyward and

were often scattered with white or colored rocks. Walls of glass, interior gardens and indoor-outdoor design continuity emphasized wide-open space. Decorative geometric cement screen walls, steel I-beams with cut outs, shapely backlit discs and starbursts, Venetian tile mosaic trim and terrazzo floors were all part of the new look. Rock accent walls provided an earthy quality and palms, split leaf philodendrons, birds of paradise and yuccas were the flora of choice. Many religious organizations found the new look heavenly and built otherworldly A-frame chapels, churches and temples. Car washes were decorated with giant spikes, spires and flags, celebrating the wash-and-wax ritual of auto beautification and the constant parade of cars in sky-high style. For these car washes, as well as motels, gas stations, coffee shops, shopping centers, dinner houses, fast-food stands and bowling alleys, towering neon and backlit plastic signs were often the finishing touch. Animated, blinking and spinning, the neons were visible from blocks away and often had big arrows pointing to the front doors.

By the late '50s Southern California's coffee shops and bowling centers were the ultimate expression of the space-age architectural trend. They were highly stylized with bright colors, dramatic and decorative lighting and had the designer

touch—even the matchbooks spoke of the future. Two local firms were the creative forces behind this extreme style. The leading architects for coffee shops were Louis Armet and Eldon Davis of Los Angeles. Their firm designed for the Denny's, Norm's, Bob's Big Boy and Huddle chains and many independents, including the Wich Stand, Romeo's Times Square and Pann's in Los Angeles and the Penguin in Santa Monica. These coffee shops offered a full menu and quick service at counters, tables and booths, often twenty-four hours a day. Their angular roofs seemed to hover above the glass walls of the dining area as the signs that projected from them drew the attention of passing motorists.

The leading bowling center designers were De Rosa, Daly & Powers of Long Beach. Their work included the Friendly Hills Bowl in Whittier, Java Lanes in Long Beach, Bowlium in Montclair, Anaheim Bowl and Covina Bowl. When AMF revolutionized the game by introducing automatic pin setters, De Rosa, Daly & Powers elevated the sport to a space-age favorite by creating bigger and better bowling alleys. More than just places to bowl, these entertainment centers were also spots to relax and socialize. Glorified with grand entrances and elaborate towering signs, the new breed of bowling alleys were deluxe twenty-four-hour sport palaces with billiard parlors, pro

shops, children's playrooms, coffee shops, dining rooms, banquet rooms and cocktail lounges. In 1955, when the Covina Bowl opened, it was the first of Southern California's new bowling center craze and the beginning of a nationwide trend.

In 1958, designer illustrations were revealed of the Theme Building, the crowning touch and centerpiece of the Los Angeles International Airport expansion. Designed to resemble a spaceship, it became a monument to a dynamic era of progress, technology and optimism, and an icon that symbolized the city of the future.

BOMB SHELTER HONEYMOON, DOWNEY, 1957. Just married, this couple made headlines when they spent their honeymoon in a backyard bomb shelter.

Los Angeles International Theme Building, illustration, 1958. A modern marvel of engineering and design, the delicate structure of the Los Angeles Airport Theme Building required more than nine hundred tons of structural steel. Construction began in April 1960 and was completed in August 1961. On the ground floor visitors entered through the Court of Stars, a series of huge color transparencies of faraway galaxies. Seventy feet above, the round, split-level "sky-high" restaurant and cocktail lounge provided patrons a bird's-eye view of airport activities. Above that, was a rooftop observation deck.

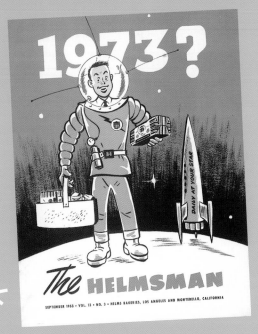

**THE HELMSMAN, SEPTEMBER 1953.**
The Helms Bakeries employee magazine featured the dream of Paul Helms, the owner: to send a loaf of Helms bread to outer space. His dream came true in 1969 when man went to the moon with a loaf of Helms bread along for the ride.

"DAIRYLAND" AT THE DRIFTWOOD DAIRY, EL MONTE, 1954. With milk carton in hand, a papier-mâché "Drifty" dressed in a space suit and sitting in a rocket, keeps a watchful eye on the school children on a field trip peering into the rotating illustrated panorama of the future at Dairyland.

GROUND-BREAKING CEREMONIES FOR DEL RIO LANES, DOWNEY, 1955. Builders and representatives of AMF, the manufacturers of the first automatic bowling pin spotters, gathered in Downey for this bowling center. When the first automatic pin-setters were installed in bowling alleys in the early '50s, they eliminated the need for human pin-spotters who were notorious for being alcoholics and contributing to the "ruffy-tuffy" reputation of bowling alleys. This led to the new "deluxe bowling centers" of the mid- and late-'50s and made bowling suburbia's favorite sport.

**ALBERTSON OLDSMOBILE DEALERSHIP, CULVER CITY, 1949.** When Oldsmobile introduced the "Rocket 88" model in 1949, the Albertson brothers built a permanent thirty-five-foot rocket as a promotional attraction and began using "Home of the Big Red Rocket" as their advertising catch phrase.

Three-eyed martians at the "Young Executives" masquerade party in an Arcadia backyard, 1956.

45

The Long Beach Elks Lodge No. 888, 1960. After years of planning and fundraising, the new Long Beach Elks Lodge was dedicated in September 1960. The enormous white flying saucer-like concrete dome was one of the most futuristic buildings ever built in Southern California. Sparsely landscaped, it was surrounded entirely by a reflecting pool lit at night with colored lights. The spacious interior was luxuriously furnished with modern décor, tropical plants and rock gardens. The Olympic-sized swimming pool, shuffleboard court, enormous deck and outdoor barbecue facilities gave the lodge a country club atmosphere.

Statler Center, Los Angeles, illustration, 1952. Part hotel, part office building, the Statler Center was a striking modern addition to the almost non-existent downtown Los Angeles skyline when it was built in 1952. With 1275 guest rooms, it was the largest hotel built in the United States in more than twenty years. Besides smart shops, cocktail lounges, public rooms, restaurants and a ballroom, there was a tropical garden café overlooking the swimming pool.

*Sky Villa Motel illustration, Pico Rivera, 1959.* "For the discriminating guest," the Sky Villa Motel featured two heated pools, room and pool service, kitchen units, executive suites, television and twenty-four-hour private phone service in every room, year-round air conditioning and the Villa Inn for "fine food and cocktails."

## Architecture

*Newport Balboa Savings, Lido Isle, Newport Beach, 1960.* Together, these bank buildings are a sampler of space-age architectural details including the rare and decorative abstract sun screen. The building on the right was built in 1954, the one on the left, 1959.

**"WELCOME TO SHIPS COFFEE SHOP . . . NEVER CLOSES," MENU COVER, 1958.** Coffee shops often used their neon signs as logo designs, but none were as timeless as the Ships menu cover. In the '50s there were two Ships Coffee Shops: Culver City, built in 1956, and Westwood, 1958.

**NORM'S ON LA CIENEGA, LOS ANGELES, 1957.** "Open 24 Hrs," Norm's Coffee Shop was designed by Armet and Davis. It epitomizes the architects' spectacular cutting-edge style of sharp rooflines hovering over walls of glass marked by a towering neon sign. The Norm's Coffee Shop chain began in Los Angeles in 1949.

Premiere Lanes, Santa Fe Springs, 1960. A sparkling array of starbursts decorate the Premiere Lanes. Bowling alley signs were often the tallest, most expensive and most elaborate signs in town.

**COVINA BOWL, 1955.** The first of the new deluxe bowling centers sparked the Southern California bowling craze, and a giant pyramid created a grand entrance. Inside there were thirty lanes, automatic pin-setting machines, a billiard room, coffee shop, restaurant, beauty salon, a nursery where the children were cared for by a registered nurse while young mothers played in housewives leagues. Its "Pyramid Room" cocktail lounge and banquet rooms were decorated with Egyptian theme murals, hieroglyphics and hand-worked copper panels depicting the arts of war.

Chapter 4

WILD WEST

The memory of those who had blazed the trails and conquered the western frontier just a few generations before was alive and well in Southern California in the 1950s. While the local aerospace and high-tech industries were leading the way to the future, nostalgia for "the good ol' days" inspired many entrepreneurs to capitalize on the homespun rustic style of the Gold Rush, western pioneers, cowboys and Indians. Western theme parks, wigwam-shaped motel rooms, genuine log cabin restaurants and chuck wagon buffets offered a warm and cozy alternative to the nostalgic space-age look of the day.

Western-themed motels, cafés, barbecue joints and restaurants took the popular suburban ranch style to the extreme. They had names such as "the Ponderosa," "the Golden Spur," "the Stage Coach Inn," and "the Trails." There were big neon signs in the shapes of covered wagons, cowboy boots and bucking broncos. Many had wood-paneled interiors and authentic décor such as old wagon wheels, hurricane lamps and stuffed wild animals. The

Westward Ho Steak House in Pasadena advertised its "authentic early California décor" in the "Palace Saloon." The Silver Saddle Inn in Downey had a huge revolving silver mounted saddle in the front window.

Western radio and television shows and movies had their heyday in the '50s. Local country and western music variety shows were toe-tappin', knee-slappin' hoedowns with sing-a-longs and square dancing. Western band leader Cliffie Stone's *Hometown Jamboree* drew capacity crowds at the Legion Stadium in El Monte where it was broadcast, as well as huge radio and television audiences. One *Jamboree* regular, Tennessee Ernie Ford, appeared on *I Love*

*Lucy* as Cousin Ernie. Hollywood cowboy superstars such as the Lone Ranger (played by Clayton Moore), Hopalong Cassidy (played by William Boyd) and Roy Rogers were superheroes in the early days of local television. Their names and images were successfully merchandised on thousands of products aimed at little boys, including toy guns, cowboy hats, bed sheets and lunch boxes. In 1951 Hopalong Cassidy became a business partner and star attraction at Hoppyland, a western-themed amusement park near Venice.

Another western star and movie stunt man, Ray "Crash" Corrigan opened Corriganville, "the world's most famous movie ranch" in Simi Valley in 1949, to offer visitors a behind-the-scenes look at western movie and TV production.

Southern California's premier tribute to the pioneers of the Old West was Knott's Berry Farm and Ghost Town. It began in 1920 when Walter and Cordelia Knott and their four children began growing berries in Buena Park. By the 1950s, the enterprising farmers had transformed their original twenty-acres into America's first western-themed amusement park. Homespun and family run, the one hundred

eighty acres of gardens, shops, amusements and Ghost Town were all created to entertain the crowds free of charge while waiting for Mrs. Knott's famous fried chicken dinner. Mrs. Knott had opened a little roadside dining room next to their berry market in 1928. She served berry pie while Mr. Knott tended the farm and sold the berries. Continually experimenting with new berry varieties, in 1932, Knott discovered a raspberry, blackberry and loganberry hybrid propagated by Rudolph Boysen, a neighboring farmer in Anaheim. Knott planted the vines and they thrived, producing big, sweet juicy berries. He named them boysenberries. To make ends meet during the Depression, in 1934, Mrs. Knott added chicken dinners to the menu. Soon the dinners required a three-hundred-seat restaurant and by 1940, she was serving as many as four thousand dinners a day. That same year, the Ghost Town opened when Walter Knott moved an abandoned hotel from an old mining town to the farm. Inside he created the farm's first historic attraction, "The

Wagon Train Panorama," a series of 3-D murals telling the story of the Knott family journey west. As the farm continued to expand, Knott daughters Marion and Toni opened a dress shop, Virginia ran a gift shop and son Russell manned the berry market. As Knott continued to expand his Ghost Town, in 1951 he bought what was left of Calico, a real ghost town in the desert east of Barstow. Saving it from completely withering away, Knott began restoring the camp as it had been in the early 1880s and officially opened it to the public. Because it was never profitable, he left Calico to the State of California as a landmark dedicated "to the memory of those who lived there long ago."

WIGWAM VILLAGE MOTEL, RIALTO, 1950. Built on Route 66, the Rialto Wigwam was the seventh and last in a chain of Wigwam Village Motels that started in Kentucky in 1937. The nineteen air-conditioned wigwams were furnished with rustic furniture and "all the modern conveniences." They surrounded a kidney-shaped swimming pool, landscaped with palms and a rambling green lawn. The marquee read, "sleep in a wigwam, get more for your wampum."

KOVER'S BULL PEN matchbook cover. Inside the matchbook cover from this Sherman Oaks eatery, a printed message reads . . . "Hy' ya, Fella, This is San Fernando Valley's most unique eating place. We serve you only the best . . . and that's no bull! Try our Sit 'n' Bull Room for firewater that'll keep your 'wigwam' . . . and they say our pies are out-of-this-world. Sincerely, Eddie Kover"

SELMA CHUCK WAGON FRANKS advertisement, LONG BEACH, 1955. A voluptuous Hollywood starlet shows off the hot dog ad on a bus bench at an open-front market.

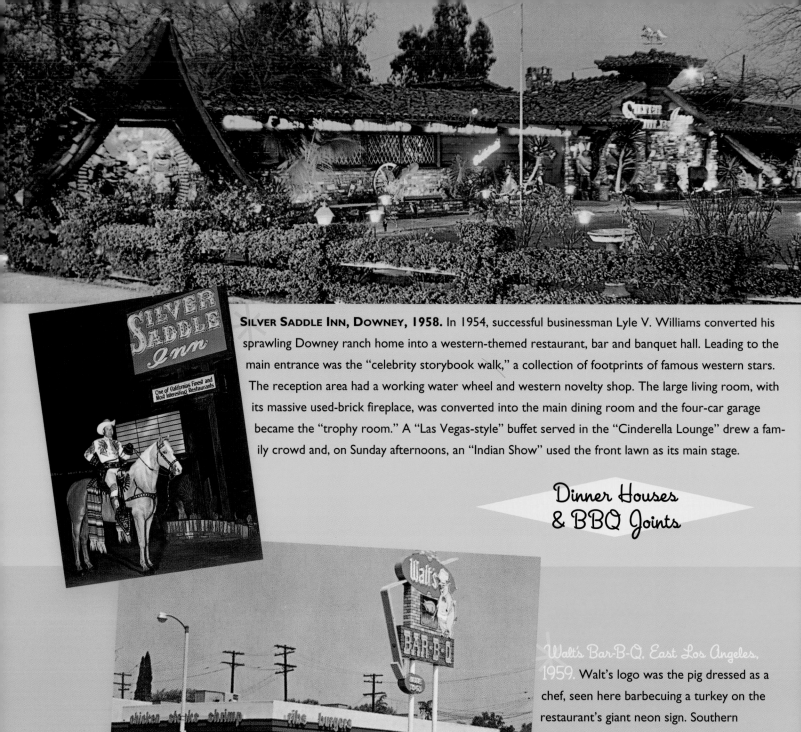

**SILVER SADDLE INN, DOWNEY, 1958.** In 1954, successful businessman Lyle V. Williams converted his sprawling Downey ranch home into a western-themed restaurant, bar and banquet hall. Leading to the main entrance was the "celebrity storybook walk," a collection of footprints of famous western stars. The reception area had a working water wheel and western novelty shop. The large living room, with its massive used-brick fireplace, was converted into the main dining room and the four-car garage became the "trophy room." A "Las Vegas-style" buffet served in the "Cinderella Lounge" drew a family crowd and, on Sunday afternoons, an "Indian Show" used the front lawn as its main stage.

*Dinner Houses & BBQ Joints*

*Walt's Bar-B-Q, East Los Angeles, 1959.* Walt's logo was the pig dressed as a chef, seen here barbecuing a turkey on the restaurant's giant neon sign. Southern Californians frequented Walt's for its "Wood Bar-B-Que with that hickory flavor" as its slogan revealed.

**CLEARMAN'S NORTH WOODS INN, MONROVIA, 1958.** A genuine log cabin set in a bed of white rock, landscaped with pine trees and decorated with giant antique logging wheels, Clearman's North Woods Inn featured a unique sign mounted on a slab cut from a thousand-year-old giant redwood tree. Inside, the atmosphere was warm and inviting with hand-carved wood beams, hurricane lamps, ceiling-mounted bearskins, risqué Gay '90s paintings and sawdust-covered floors littered with peanut shells. The bartenders in the rustic cocktail lounge wore plaid vests and string ties, while waitresses wore plaid scooped neck can-can costumes with regulation high heels and red nail polish. The menu included cocktails, "lumberjack-sized" sandwiches. Later fake snow was added to the roof. In the late 1960s when the freeway was built through Monrovia, the restaurant was dismantled log by log and rebuilt at Clearman's Village in Rosemead.

**JACK'S BULL PIT BARBECUE, LAGUNA BEACH, 1956.** Cowhide booths and hundreds of cattle brands on the walls lent authentic western style to Jack's, whose ads proudly announced, "All of our meats are cooked in the pit with wood only."

55

## Children's boat ride, Hoppyland, near Venice, 1953.

Originally called Venice Lake Park when it opened in 1950, the name of the eighty-acre amusement park was changed to Hoppyland in 1951, when world famous western and TV star Hopalong Cassidy, a.k.a. actor William Boyd, became a business partner. Located along the Ballona Wetlands near Venice, the Venice Wranglers played western music and Hoppy himself made personal appearances. With popular Hopalong Cassidy toys, guns, western clothes and souvenirs selling in the gift shop. Hoppyland featured several pony rides, more than twenty thrill rides, a mini roller coaster called the Little Dipper, a double Ferris wheel, a kiddyland and a miniature railroad that circled the park. As appealing to adults as it was to the little ones, Hoppyland featured evening dances around the turn-of-the-century carousel, picnic grounds, baseball diamonds, horseshoe-pitching lanes and a lake for swimming, boating and a water skiing show with a legless skier. In 1954, after being open for only three years, the park was closed to make way for the world's largest small craft harbor, Marina Del Rey.

## Grizzly Flats Railroad, San Gabriel, early '50s.

America's first privately owned and operated full-scale backyard railroad, Grizzly Flats Railroad began in 1939 when Ward Kimball and his wife Betty rescued an 1881 steam train from the scrap heap and brought it to their rural ranch in San Gabriel. Kimball, an Academy Award winner and one of Walt Disney's top animators, meticulously restored the old train. Soon he began restoring and adding more rolling stock to his unique collection. The Kimballs often hosted costume parties that included "an excursion over the great pleasure route of the Grizzly Flats RR, the scenic wonder of the West." Walt Disney, Kimball's boss and fellow train enthusiast, was often on the guest list. By the '50s the railroad had three steam engines, a passenger coach, a cattle car, a flat-bottom gondola, a side-door caboose and a train station furnished with authentic railroad heirlooms. The Grizzly Flats Railroad station was a gift to the Kimballs from Walt Disney after it was used as a set for the 1949 Disney film, *So Dear to My Heart*. In 1955, the station was used as a model for the Frontierland train station at Disneyland Park.

**Corriganville, Simi Valley, 1952.**
Spectators watch as western movie star and daredevil stuntman Ray "Crash" Corrigan, left, and one of his movie buddies stage a live-action western stunt show at Corriganville. This western movie-and-television set and amusement park and stunt show opened to the public on May 1, 1949. For one dollar per carload, visitors could see mountain trails, caves, a Mexican Village, Robin Hood's lake and forest (named for the *Robin Hood* movie that was filmed there), a fortress and the little Main Street called Silvertown—all movie sets. There were rodeos, pony rides, stagecoach rides, horses for rent and even a chance to see a western movie being filmed. Five-cent salami sandwiches were served along with draft beer or sarsaparilla in the Silver Dollar Saloon while western music was piped through loudspeakers. Corrigan purchased the rural two-thousand-acre site in 1938 believing he might locate a Spanish treasure rumored to be buried in the rugged terrain. After finding nothing, he decided to make more "gold" by renting the ranch as a western movie location. During the '40s and '50s, hundreds of westerns were filmed there. In 1957, Jack Wrather, the owner of the *Lone Ranger* TV series, gained control over the park and changed the name to Lone Ranger Ranch. In 1958, Corrigan sued and regained control and changed the name back to Corriganville. In 1966, Corriganville was purchased by Bob Hope and it became "Hopetown."

*Calico Souvenir Booklet, 1952.* It tells readers, "This book is dedicated to the memory of the heroic Silver Pioneers whose daring and toil created Southern California's greatest Silver Camp, Calico."

## Calico Ghost Town

*Calico ghost town, 1957.* Three generations pause to have their picture taken during their visit to this authentic ghost town, an old mining camp in the desert east of Barstow. Once Southern California's greatest silver camp, in the 1880s prospectors mined eighty-seven million dollars worth of silver from the colorful hills. In 1896, silver was devalued and the mines were shut down. Overnight the location known for one of the most valuable silver ore discoveries ever recorded was suddenly deserted.

Inspired by his passion for the old towns and pioneers of the Gold Rush days, during the '40s and the '50s Walter Knott's ghost town grew into a well-researched environment of authentic buildings, interiors, demonstrations, interactive displays, heirlooms, memorabilia and transportation from the Old West. There was a schoolhouse, blacksmith shop, Chinese laundry, cemetery and jail with a "talking" mannequin, inmate "Sad Eye Joe." Dance hall girls did the can-can in the Calico Saloon and melodramas were performed in the Birdcage Theater. The general store offered soda pop and sarsaparilla and a warm spot to sit around the pot-bellied stove. Quaint shops sold antiques, flowers, rocks, books, handmade crafts, souvenirs, candy and boysenberry jam. An Indian Trading Post, a little chapel and a nondenominational church sat beside a lake. After the sun went down, a giant campfire roared in the Wagon Camp where there was storytelling, square dancing and live western music.

Knott's Berry Farm

The Ghost Town & Calico Railroad, 1951. Passengers wait to board an authentic Colorado mining train that was moved to Knott's Berry Farm in 1951. Other tours around the amusement park included horse-and-buggy rides, stagecoach trips, pack mules and a tram.

Cecilia and Marilyn, 1954. The ghost town's two most photographed women pose with an admirer.

**KNOTT CHARACTERS, 1954.**

Walter Knott populated his ghost town with employees and mannequins dressed in authentic period costumes as prospectors, cowboys and Indians, townspeople and chorus girls.

Young visitors play dress up and pose with Native Americans, 1954.

Panning for gold in Knott's Gold Mine, 1954. This authentic creation of a typical 1849 California gold mine meant that for twenty-five cents Ghost Town visitors could pan for actual gold nuggets with the expert help of old prospectors. Knott stocked the sluice boxes with ten thousand dollars worth of gold every year.

STEAK HOUSE
IN GHOST TOWN
◄ KNOTT'S BERRY FARM ►
BUENA PARK - CALIFORNIA
TELEPHONE • BUENA PARK: LAWRENCE 2-1131

GET A 25¢ TICKET AT THE
SHACK and PAN OUT YOUR
OWN GOLD
THE MINER WILL SHOW YOU HOW

KNOTT'S STEAK HOUSE MENU COVER, 1959. An alternative to Mrs. Knott's legendary chicken dinner, the Steak House was decorated with Indian chiefs' portraits and authentic Native American artifacts.

**THE HAUNTED SHACK, 1957.** "The key to this mystery lies forever buried with the shack's original owners, Shanty Sam and his wife Shaky Sadie" said the brochure explaining this magical cabin where water flowed backwards, balls rolled uphill and people grew a foot taller. Visitors couldn't stand up straight in the Ghost Town's most unusual attraction, which made the Haunted Shack all the eerier. Knott discovered the Haunted Shack in Nevada and moved it completely intact to the Ghost Town.

Chapter 5

FOREIGN FLAIR

Southern California was a United Nations of foreign-themed environments, restaurants and shops. With international flights still an expensive proposition, typical Southern Californians had not traveled outside the USA, so adding foreign flair to

commercial enterprises helped bring a desirable sense of worldly sophistication to the locals. But the décor of the Orient, South Seas, Old World and South of the Border was often taken to whimsical and theatrical extremes. Coupled with an innocent make-believe quality, these foreign-themed businesses often suggested a fairytale adventure to another world, with little authentic relationship to their faraway inspirations.

New Chinatown and Olvera Street, both in downtown Los Angeles, were among the area's most popular and most publicized tourist attractions. Olvera Street was Southern California's original pedestrian mall. Lined with some of the city's most historic buildings, the block-long street was closed to vehicular traffic in 1930 and converted to an open-air Mexican marketplace. Celebrated as the oldest street in Los Angeles, Olvera Street was restored as a place "to pre-

serve and present the customs and trades of early California." A 1950s tour brochure promoted it as "a must-see attraction of taco shacks, outdoor cafés, nightclubs, strolling mariachis, fortune tellers, stalls and shops selling hand-crafted Mexican wares, all operated by Mexicans in their native costume." New Chinatown, built in 1938 just after Union Station was built on the site of the old Chinatown, was promoted in the 1950s as "an Oriental oasis of quaint souvenir shops, selling oriental oddities, souvenirs, silks, jewelry and clothing, Chinese restaurants and nightclubs and a dimly lit perfumed temple."

Little Tokyo, also in downtown Los Angeles, and Solvang, in Santa Barbara County, were not promoted in the 1950s as tourist attractions. Unlike Chinatown, Little Tokyo was not heavily adorned with oriental architectural details. The community of Little Tokyo began just after the turn of the century when Japanese-Americans were recruited in northern California by Henry Huntington to lay tracks for the Pacific Electric Railway. In the

early '50s, one-fourth of Little Tokyo's commercial frontage and housing for nearly a thousand people was demolished to build Parker Center, the new Los Angeles Police Department headquarters. Solvang, a charming Danish village built in the architectural style of old Denmark, wasn't discovered as a major tourist attraction until the late 1950s when the town's leading bakery, Birkholm's, put up a billboard on nearby Highway 101. Soon the quaint town of Old World architecture, windmills, cobblestone streets and gas street lamps was catering to the tourist trade.

French, Mexican, Chinese and Italian restaurants, Dutch bakeries, Swedish *smorgasbords,* German *hofbraus* and old English and Irish pubs, served up an around-the-world tour of "authentic cuisine and décor," authenticity that soon

became cultural cliches. Pizza parlors, spaghetti houses and Italian restaurants, such as the Italian Kitchen in downtown Los Angeles, typically had red-and-white checkered tablecloths and plenty of empty Chianti bottles. Bit of Sweden in Hollywood was promoted as "the world's largest smorgasbord." The motto at El Gordo, a Mexican restaurant in San Gabriel, was "home of the 'beeg theek' steaks." At Balalaika, a Russian restaurant in Hollywood, "Chicken a la Moscow" was the specialty of the house. The Queens Arms, a medieval-themed dinner house in Encino, served the "Flaming Swords Buffet" in "Ye Round Table Room." A neon Eiffel Tower decorated the rooftop at Marcel and Jeanne's French Café in Montebello.

By far, the most popular theme for shops and restaurants the 1950s was the exotic style of tropical South Seas islands. The Sea and Jungle Imports shop in Glendale, which specialized in "complete Polynesian décor" for homes, parties, restaurants, commercial displays including black lighting, waterfalls and tiki bars, claimed to be "the largest store of its kind in the world." Many Polynesian restaurants, such as The Hawaiian in Long Beach, Sam's Seafood in Huntington Beach and the Bali Hai on Shelter Island in San Diego, had Polynesian floor shows and luau-style parties.

In the late 1950s, from the glorified flapjack to one of the most ambitious developments ever imagined in Southern California, there was a new concept in international foreign-themed menus, shops and environments.

Aunt Emma's Round the World Pancake House in Newport Beach and San Diego served "pancake recipes from every continent . . . Germany, Sweden, Hawaii, Africa, Holland and France." The International House of Pancakes followed suit and served similar recipes. In 1959, the city of Orange in Orange County announced ambitious plans to build International Marketland, a shopping center, special events exhibit hall and hotel complex. Developers promoted it as a "joyous place where a hundred different countries can own a hundred different shops in the same marketplace and a joyous adventure in shopping, dining, exhibits and attractions sponsored and operated by the nations they depict." The visual icon of the proposed marketplace was to be the "World Sphere," a translucent plastic half-globe three hundred feet in diameter. Recreations of famous buildings representing many foreign lands were planned. The finishing touch was to be an enormous helium-filled globe balloon floating high in the sky attached by an adjustable tether and visible from miles around. As prosperous as the times were, ultimately this extreme development was never realized.

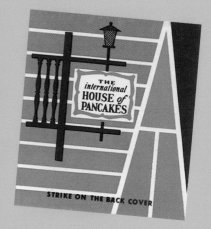

*Olvera Street watercolor painting, 1954. Olvera Street was the favorite downtown destination for tourists eager for some lively Mexican entertainment and shopping. Near Union Station, the colorful collection of shops and restaurants was built on the original Plaza de Los Angeles.*

**BIRKHOLM'S BAKERY IN SOLVANG, 1959.** Known as "the bakery that made Solvang famous," Birkholm's opened in 1951. As in many of the businesses in this quaint Danish community north of Santa Barbara, the employees wore colorful native costumes.

Old World

*Van de Kamp's Windmill Bakery, Los Angeles area, early '50s.*

The Van de Kamp's Dutch Bakery began in Los Angeles in 1921 and expanded with each store marked by a revolving windmill. In the early '50s the bakery had expanded into a coffee shop and drive-in restaurant business and the quaint little corner windmill bakery stores were on their way out. During the '50s, the bakery items were sold inside small shops in local supermarkets; each "supermarket store" had a revolving blue neon windmill sign hung near its entrance.

**THE "CAFÉ DE CHAMPS ELYSÉES BAR" AT ROBAIRE'S, LOS ANGELES, 1957.**

An enormous photo mural of Paris covered the wall and provided a dramatic backdrop for the hot pink bar stools, upholstered bar and scalloped awning in this favorite French restaurant. The advertising slogan was "If you like Paris, you'll love Robaire's."

✳ "New Chinatown," 1956. Many of the restaurants in Chinatown advertised authentic Cantonese food, yet they served chop suey, sweet and sour pork and Peking duck, dishes unknown in China.

✳ Golden Pagoda Restaurant, Chinatown, Los Angeles, early '50s. The crowning touch to "New Chinatown," the Golden Pagoda was built in 1941. During the 1950s it was promoted as "the most distinctive and colorfully decorated Chinese restaurant in Los Angeles," and it was. The specialty of the cocktail lounge was the "Pagoda Delight."

Golden Dragon Bar at the Chungking Café, Anaheim, 1959.
Typical of many of Southern California's Chinese restaurants in
the '50s, the "Oriental" theme was taken to the extreme.

The Orient

Kona Kai Motel, Anaheim, 1959. Typical of the cookie-cutter rock-roofed motels in Southern California, this two-story motel was glorified with a name and décor that suggested a faraway place.

The Luau, Beverly Hills, 1953. Opened by Steven Crane, a one-time B-movie actor and second husband of 1940s and '50s screen goddess Lana Turner, the Luau was a reincarnation of an earlier popular Polynesian restaurant called Sugie's Tropics, which occupied the same site on Rodeo Drive. Inside, the exotic décor included rattan fan chairs, tropical plants and flowers and a waterfall flowing into a stream that meandered through the dining room.

*Souvenir photograph, Clifton's Pacific Seas Cafeteria, downtown Los Angeles, 1956.* The roving souvenir photographer in the Clifton's dining room memorialized many tourists' trips to the cafeteria. Opened in 1931, the interior was heavily detailed with enormous painted tropical murals, blond bamboo, rock grottos, thatched huts and five giant neon tropical bouquets. In 1960, Clifton's Pacific Seas closed to make room for a parking lot.

*Tiki Gods & Tiki Torches*

*The Traders, Beverly Hills, 1955.* Opened in 1956, The Traders was part of the Trader Vic's restaurant chain and later was renamed Trader Vic's. According to the original press release, "The Traders is decorated like the temple room of an ancient Maori ceremonial hut." And, also of note, "an employee of the Beverly Hills Phone Company was commissioned to hand-carve the eight decorative tiki gods."

International Marketland, rendering for the city of Orange, 1959. The proposed International Marketland featured recreations of the leaning Tower of Pisa, an Egyptian pyramid, a Moorish mosque and the Parthenon of Athens. Though never built, the foreign design featured a proposed high-rise department store, a skyscraper international hotel and the "World Sphere," a translucent plastic dome designed to represent the northern hemisphere and to house a "foreign department store."

**Chapter 6**

# ANIMAL ATTRACTIONS

In the '50s, the world famous San Diego Zoo had the largest collection of wild animals anywhere and the Los Angeles Zoo was plagued with controversy. Novelty animal acts were a staple of local television, and Lassie was one of Hollywood's biggest

77

for the downtrodden, it represented a bit of hope.

In 1952, The Jungle, one of the world's largest privately owned zoos, opened in Anaheim. The star attraction was Jerry "the world's most human chimpanzee." A year before, eccentric millionaire and showman Jack Dutton and his wife Dorothy had "adopted" a wild chimpanzee to add to their ever-expanding collection of birds and other unusual pets. They kept the unique menagerie at their rural ranch home in Fullerton. They named the chimp Jerry and raised him as their child. Within a few months he was toilet trained, ate at the dinner table, dressed himself and even slept in the same bed with the Duttons. He began entertaining at birthday parties and local Orange County events. When nagging neighbors continued to complain about the wild pet "monkey" and all the other pets, Dutton bought a five-acre orange grove in nearby Anaheim where he built a showcase for Jerry and all of the other pets so the public could enjoy them. He transformed the property into a lush tropical wonderland by planting hundreds of palm trees from six different countries and tropical plants from every

stars. Jayne Mansfield made "special celebrity appearances" with her pet poodle at dog shows. A midget vs. kangaroo boxing match helped sell washing machines and refrigerators in Pomona. And Jerry "the world's most human chimpanzee" went berserk in Anaheim. Southern California was, indeed, attracted to animals.

But animals had long been curiosities in the area. In 1910, for instance, prehistoric bones were found at La Brea Tar Pits, indicating that the terrain had been home to Ice Age mammals long extinct. Coupled with the reptiles at the California Alligator Farm, the Tar Pits quickly became one of Los Angeles's two leading tourist attractions. By the 1920s, the San Diego and Los Angeles Zoos had been opened, and by the '30s, movie star lions and tigers and bears were on display at Jungleland in Thousand Oaks. By the '40s, horse racing at Santa Anita, Del Mar and Hollywood Park was a favorite pastime of the rich and the famous and continent. Jerry shared his new home with snakes, alligators, elephants, bears, ostriches, deer, spider monkeys, apes, a lion and hundreds of exotic birds. Locals, tourists, schoolchildren and church groups enjoyed Jerry's antics as he played with Sunny the bear or swam with the ducks in the pond. "Jerry amused the guests in the daytime and helped me water the plants and feed the other animals at night," Dutton explained. Admission was free and The Jungle was an instant success. Dutton added a restaurant, luau garden, gift shop, beauty shop and barbershop. By the time nearby Disneyland opened in 1955 and took the spotlight away from The Jungle, things were beginning to get out of hand. Late-night pranksters taunted the animals and thieves stole the flamingos. A series of lawsuits forced Dutton to sell his "dangerous" animals, and his wife ran off with his lawyer. Even Jerry wasn't safe. Having grown accustomed to his freedom in the jungle, the "humanized" chimp needed too much supervision and went berserk when he was put in his cage. Caretakers were hired to baby-sit Jerry around the clock. Dutton then reluctantly offered his beloved pet chimp to zoos, but none would take him. When Jerry became more and more impossible, Dutton took Jerry into a nearby orange grove and gave him a shovel. "I had him dig a deep hole," Dutton said, "when he was fin-

ished, I told him to jump inside. Then a policeman friend of mine shot him in the head." A less human chimp replaced Jerry and The Palms restaurant became the star attraction.

In 1958 the *Los Angeles Daily News* called the city zoo in Griffith Park an "inadequate, ugly, poorly designed and underfinanced collection of beat-up cages." After years of problems and controversy—it had long been considered by many in the zoological community to be the worst zoo in a major city in the country—local voters overwhelmingly approved a bond issue to build a new "Los Angeles World Zoo." Expectations were high. One newspaper headline predicted that it would be the biggest zoo in the world. The political and legal battle for control of the new zoo quickly spawned a media circus. Roy Rogers proposed running the zoo as a Wild West park and selling sponsorship to a television network. There was even controversy over the new zoo's location. The first proposed site was Elysian Park near downtown, then Pacoima, and finally back to Griffith Park. Golfers were irate because the Roosevelt golf course at the northeast end of the park was to be eliminated. After much political hullabaloo, the groundbreaking ceremony for the new zoo finally took place in 1964.

JERRY

"SPEED," SAN DIEGO ZOO, 1959. The ironically named 526-pound tortoise was a century old when he gave two kids a ride at the San Diego Zoo. By the '50s, the zoo had long been considered one of the finest in the world. It had expanded to two hundred subtropical acres and was home to more than 3,200 animals, many of the rarest in captivity, including the only koala outside Australia. The zoo began unexpectedly when animals imported for the 1915 California Panama Exhibition were quarantined and had to stay. In 1955, a local television show called *Zoorama* made its debut.

Jack Dutton and his beloved Jerry, The Jungle, 1954. In happier times, the owner posed with his childlike chimp.

**THE JUNGLE SIGNPOST, 1953.** The restaurant at The Jungle, The Palms, began as a Japanese teahouse-style snack bar but quickly grew into a full restaurant and "genuine luau garden" large enough to accommodate seven hundred guests. The restaurant's catch phrase was "dine in the spell of the tropics." Cantonese and American cuisines were served amid live palms trees in the Terrace Room and exotic wood carvings from all over the world in the Gold Room. The Lantern cocktail lounge was decorated with a rare collection of imported lanterns and featured live Polynesian entertainment, dancing and a one-time performance by Eartha Kitt. The beauty salon was called the Head Hunters, and the gift shop sold Hawaiian clothing, exotic curios and luau party supplies.

The Jungle

**JERRY OF THE JUNGLE, 1954.** A chimp with human qualities, Jerry was the main draw at the animal park, then met an unthinkable death.

Jerry, the official portrait, 1954. "The world's most human chimpanzee."

Trainers Jo and James Madison, pose with "20 tons of pachyderms."

## Jungleland

**JUNGLELAND, THOUSAND OAKS, 1959.**

Jungleland began in Thousand Oaks in 1929. The owner, Hollywood lion tamer Louis Goebel, began training lions in the early '20s working at the original Gay's Lion Farm in Hollywood. In 1926, He purchased six lions that were being sold by Universal Studios. Unable to find affordable property in Los Angeles County where he could board the lions, he built his lion farm, Jungleland, in Thousand Oaks. In the '50s it was promoted as the home of film and TV animal stars including Leo, the MGM Lion. Other Jungleland attractions included "wild" animal shows, jungle rides, baby zoo and Monkey Island.

Official program, Hollywood Park, 1955. "The Track of the Lake and Flowers" opened in 1938 in Inglewood. Hollywood Park was owned and operated by the Hollywood Turf Club whose members included film stars, directors and producers, including Al Jolson, Bing Crosby, Jack Warner, Sam Goldwyn, Darryl Zanuck and Walt Disney. In 1958, Hollywood Park hosted "Huck Finn Day" in its beautifully landscaped infield. Conceived by Inglewood's Chief of Police as an idea to "improve juvenile public relations," boys and girls were admitted only if they were wearing Huck Finn-type clothing. Boys came a la Huck Finn and girls came as Becky Thatcher. Bamboo fishing rods were handed out and the kids fished in the bass-stocked infield lakes. Prizes were given for the best costumes, longest fish and the biggest catch of the day.

**DEL MAR RACETRACK, NORTH OF SAN DIEGO, EARLY '50s.** Opened in 1937, Del Mar was co-owned by Bing Crosby who recorded the song that would open and close every day of racing, "Where the Turf Meets the Surf." Other celebrity regulars included Jimmy Durante and Lucille Ball and Desi Arnaz.

*At the Races*

**SANTA ANITA PARK, ARCADIA, 1951.** Dressing up for a day at the races was de rigueur as these three ladies prove, posed before one of the many spectacular floral displays at "The Winter-Spring Capital of the Finest Thoroughbred Racing in the Country." Opened in 1934, the race rack was famous for its infield display of flowers and spectacular views of the Sierra Madre Mountains.

**LA BREA TAR PITS, LOS ANGELES, 1955.** One of the area's earliest tourist attractions, the redundantly named La Brea Tar Pits were discovered in 1905 as the world's largest collection of Ice Age fossils. The animals and their predators were trapped in the bubbling pools of tar millions of years before. When the land was donated to Los Angeles County in 1915, collectors had already taken over six thousand bones from the site. By the '50s, the tar pits and the surrounding preserve were landscaped like a typical city park and in the middle of one of the city's most fashionable shopping districts, Miracle Mile.

Midget vs. kangaroo boxing match, Agitator Appliance Shop in Pomona, 1959. A wild and crazy in-store promotion and mixed-up boxing exhibition helped sell stoves and refrigerators. Man vs. grizzly bear wrestling matches were also a crowd pleaser at promotional events.

*California Alligator Farm, Buena Park, 1953.* Visitors watch one of the trained "movie star" alligators on the water slide at the Alligator Farm, across the street from Knott's Berry Farm. "Alligator Joe" Campbell, the owner, began collecting and exhibiting alligators in Hot Springs, Arkansas, before the turn of the twentieth century. In 1907, he transported his exotic reptile collection on special railroad cars from their native land to Southern California. Soon the snakes, lizards, turtles, crocodiles and alligators were a popular Los Angeles tourist attraction in Lincoln Park and one of the world's largest reptile collections. There were trained alligator and snake shows where spitting cobras stunned the crowds. Baby alligators hatched from their eggs in incubators while on full public view. The largest crocodile in captivity snapped whole fish and chicken tossed to him by his keepers. Some of the reptiles were trained and appeared in movies. In 1953, Campbell's grandson took over the business and moved the entire reptile population to new, more spacious quarters: two acres in Buena Park.

# Chapter 7

# DESERT DELIGHTS

Southern California's desert was a hotbed of activity in the '50s. Palm Springs was the most famous desert resort town in the world, Indio was the date capital of the USA, Apple Valley was a new town dedicated to "happy, healthy living," and the

Salton Sea was being sold as *the* new place to live and have fun. Developers, speculators and the rich and famous built new housing developments, recreational facilities, exclusive private clubs, resort hotels, motels and trailer parks, all made endurable with swimming pools and air conditioning. Many new tourists came for just a visit and never left. Some tourists became regular seasonal resort guests and many bought second homes. Desert style was low and spread out. The motif varied from modern and ranch to a bit of exotica. The dress code was casual and there was always plenty of time for outdoor sports, horseback rid-ing, swimming and lounging in the sun.

The elite began developing Palm Springs as a summery winter playground getaway in the '20s. By 1950, the fash-ionable oasis was in its heyday: smart shops, chic restaurants, private clubs, fancy motels, resort hotels, designer homes, elegant sporting and social events. There were new places to go and each one was the "in spot" for at least a moment, some even longer. During The Season (from October to June) the biggest names in show business mixed and mingled with the jet set and everyday upper-crust folk. Lucille Ball and Desi Arnaz,

Frank Sinatra, Dean Martin, Bob Hope, Bing Crosby, Jack Benny, Dinah Shore, Liberace and Zsa Zsa Gabor all built spectacular sprawling homes. Lavishly decorated with up-to-date designer fur-nishings, the domains were generously plotted on golf courses and rocky moun-tainsides. The most unique desert retreat was built by millionaire manufac-turer and inventor of the gas-powered chain saw, Robert McCulloch. An ultra-modern push-button paradise of built-in mechanical gadgets that automatically poured cocktails at the bar, opened the drapes, played soft music, filled the bath-tub and flashed a red light in the kitchen to tell the but-ler to bring coffee, McCulloch's home was otherwise of classic desert design: a mix of glass, ter-razzo and rare woods. Outside, beside the swim-ming pool, waterfalls, ten-nis courts and nine-hole miniature golf course, revolved a human-sized Lazy Susan with seven chaise longues arranged on a round pedestal that slowly turned to insure an even tan.

On a regular basis, the luxurious resorts of Palm Springs offered

chuck wagon breakfasts, swimming, tennis, badminton, Ping-Pong, croquet, shuffleboard, cards, horseback riding and health clubs. Poolside barbecues and fish fries, brunches, buffets, designer fashion shows, themed western and luau costume parties, moonlight hay rides, dining and dancing, orchestras and celebrity entertainers. Palm Springs had more swimming pools per capita than any other city in the nation and golf replaced tennis as the desert's most popular sport. In 1951, The Thunderbird Golf Course and Country Club opened near Palm Springs and started a new desert trend of private, member-owned clubs that bordered golf courses with luxurious homes, swimming pools, tennis courts and clubhouses. Members traveled the beautifully landscaped grounds in golf carts and paid up to $100,000 to join. In 1954, Lucille Ball and Desi Arnaz built a home on the Thunderbird grounds but because of his Latin heritage, Arnaz was not invited to join the country club. So he built his own: the Desi Arnaz Western Hills Hotel. At the 1957 groundbreaking ceremony he told the press "We won't discriminate against gentiles, Jews or Cubans."

There were more than five thousand acres of date palms in the Coachella Valley supplying ninety percent of the nation's dates. Many of the date farmers along the roads between Palm Springs and Indio had roadside shops at the edge of their groves. Each tried to outdo the other with special date gift packs and crystallized, candied, brandied, stuffed and dipped dates, as well as handmade date cookies, cakes, ice creams and milkshakes.

In the late '50s, fast talking salesmen began selling the Salton Sea as California's "American Mediterranean," a wonderland of water sports, fishing and hunting. New communities called Salton Riviera, Salton City and Bombay Beach were planned and promised with utopian homes, marinas, motels, parks, playgrounds and golf courses. Prospective residents were brought in by the busload. The sales pitch often included luau parties, beauty contests and speedboat races, which helped to create publicity. Initially the response was good, but ultimately most of the plans were never realized.

Apple Valley, high in the Mojave Desert, had very few residents when two retired oil millionaires from Long Beach began developing and promoting it in 1946 as "California's only all year Desert Resort Playground." They proposed a perfectly planned community with beautiful ranch homes, modern schools and shops, wide roads and bridle paths, a golf course, an airfield and an impressive inn for guests and visitors. By the early '50s, it had all come true.

LONE PALM HOTEL. PALM SPRINGS, 1957. Bandleader Horace Heidt's twin sons, Jerry and Jack, greet guests at their father's famed Lone Palm Hotel resort.

THE DOLL HOUSE MATCHBOOK, EARLY '50s. Opened in 1945, the Doll House was the *other* hot night spot in Palm Springs throughout the 1950s. A great place for star gazing, the Doll House earned its reputation. Common advice at the time was "when you get to Palm Springs, stop at the Doll House. If no one is there, no one's in Palm Springs."

*Apple Valley Inn, artist's rendering, 1953.* Located in the Mojave Desert ninety-three miles from Los Angeles, the Apple Valley Inn opened in 1948. By 1950 it was one of the most famous resort hotels in the country. Jeff Chandler, Errol Flynn, Hedda Hopper and Marilyn Monroe were all guests The price per person with two to a room for seven days, six nights and eighteen meals was seventy-eight dollars. Daytime activities included golf, horseback riding, horseshoes, archery, Ping-Pong, tennis, shuffleboard, swimming and card tournaments. Each evening there was dancing and entertainment in the Gay '90s Western Bar. There were weekly midnight wiener-roast pool parties with cowboy songs around the campfire, chuck wagon fried-steak dinners, poolside buffets and square dancing. During the first years of operation, the fifty guest cottages didn't have phones due to the limited phone service to the rural community. They were each equipped with carrier pigeons to send their room service orders to the kitchen. The guests would attach their order to the pigeon's leg and let it loose. When the room service waiter arrived with the order, he would bring back the pigeon.

*Apple Valley Inn, Christmas day, 1950. A well-to-do Glendale family spending the holiday season in the Mojave Desert poses for a poolside portrait.*

*Apple Valley Inn brochure, 1955. Newt was a caricature of one of the oil millionaires, Newton Bass.*

Apple Valley Inn

Salton Sea North Shore Beach and Yacht Club entrance, 1960. Unique by any modern architectural standards, the North Shore Beach and Yacht Club was a high-tech combination of pink concrete block, green fiberglass and corrugated aluminum with hooded port-hole windows. It had a rooftop observation deck, dining room and the Commodore Room cocktail lounge.

Salton Sea

Desert Garden Motel, Salton City, 1959. Advertised as *the* Salton Sea headquarters for the hunter, boater, water skier, fisherman and "rockhound," Desert Garden Motel greeted visitors arriving by plane at the nearby airport and instructed them to buzz the motel for transportation from the airport.

Shields Date Garden billboard, 1959. The word "sex" on a billboard was taboo in the 1950s. Mr. Shields knew this would attract curiosity seekers who would have to pass through the date shop to get to the "Romance Theater" to see what it was all about.

## Shields Date Garden

Shields Date Garden, between Palm Springs and Indio, 1953. Founded in 1924, by 1950 when the new salesroom and Romance Theater were built, the Shields Date Farm offered 119 different types of dates including its own "blonde" and "brunette" varieties. Visitors were invited to take a walk through the date grove and tour the packing house.

**THE RACQUET CLUB, PALM SPRINGS, 1956.** A '56 Cadillac convertible parked poolside at the Palm Springs Racquet Club. One of the earliest resorts in Palm Springs, the Racquet Club remained one of the town's most fashionable places to see and be seen throughout the decade.

*The Clubs*

**PALM SPRINGS TENNIS CLUB, 1952.** A well-to-do Long Beach woman poses poolside at the picturesque Palm Springs Tennis Club. The club promoted its beautiful oval swimming pool as the most photographed pool in the Springs.

Lucille Ball and Desi Arnaz, Thunderbird Country Club, 1955. Lucy and Desi in the doorway of their six-bedroom, six-bathroom home at the Thunderbird. When the exclusive club didn't invite Arnaz to join, he spent a million dollars to build his own country club.

## Desi Arnaz Western Hills Hotel

Poolside, Desi Arnaz Western Hills Hotel, 1957. The desert's only hotel built on a golf course, it had forty-two rooms and suites furnished, according to the brochure, with "all the latest innovations: television, refrigeration cooling, private lanais and personal cocktail bars."

The Desi Arnaz Western Hills Hotel, 1957. An accordionist, bass player and vocalist perform to a packed house in the Sunken Bar at the Western Hills Hotel. Featured on the cocktail menu were drinks from Desi's personal Cuban repertoire. The house orchestra was the band that toured the country with Desi before he began *I Love Lucy* in 1951.

## Desert Air Hotel

**Compass Room Restaurant, Desert Air Hotel, 1951.** The Desert Air added the round Compass Room and the Luau Hut cocktail lounge, both decorated in a tropical motif.

**Desert Air brochure, Palm Springs, 1958.** Built in 1946, the Desert Air was Palm Springs' only fly-in resort, thus its slogan, "fly in . . . drive in." The two 3200-foot grass landing strips were capable of accepting any private or chartered plane. Moonlight airplane rides were among the long list of recreational activities offered.

PALM SPRINGS, CALIFORNIA

FLY IN---

*Desert Air*

HOTEL AND COTTAGES

---DRIVE IN

-DESERT AIR HOTEL-

## The Chi Chi

**Chi Chi, Palm Springs, 1954.** Called "the showplace of the desert," the Chi Chi was the desert's biggest, fanciest and most popular nightspot. During the '50s, headliners in the Starlite Room included Nat King Cole, Louis Armstrong, Dorothy Dandridge, Patti Page, Peggy Lee, Edgar Bergen and Charlie McCarthy, Sophie Tucker and Ella Fitzgerald. Celebrity members of the audience often joined the star for impromptu performances.

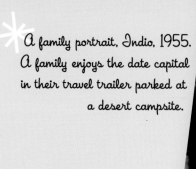

*A family portrait, Indio, 1955. A family enjoys the date capital in their travel trailer parked at a desert campsite.

*Shriners convention, El Mirador Hotel, Palm Springs, 1959. Mobil Oil executives don their fezzes.

Fun in the Sun

*Tamarisk Country Club, Palm Springs, 1955. A golfer in matching lavender golf duds and golf cart.

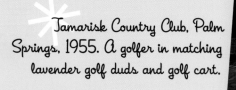

# Chapter 8

# HIGH ALTITUDES

About one hundred miles from the Pacific Ocean, the sport of snow skiing was growing faster in the San Bernardino mountains of Southern California than anywhere else in the country in the 1950s. Quaint mountain resort areas were promoted as

SAN BERNARDINO
Mountain
Resort Area

fun for everyone

SPRING
SUMMER
FALL
WINTER

"the ideal family vacation-land, America's favorite all year playground," and "perfect for the active sportsman or the sight-seer seeking relaxation." Santa and Mrs. Claus were the newest and most famous mountain residents. They set up shop in Santa's Village, a Christmas-themed amusement park near Lake Arrowhead, complete with Dancer, Prancer, Donder and Blitzen.

The communities of Big Bear, Lake Arrowhead, Idyllwild and Mt. Baldy were rustic campsites just before the turn of the twentieth century. During the '50s, they began expanding rapidly with new taverns, lodges, inns, guest ranches, motels, trailer courts and campsites to suit every style and budget. Many people built mountain cabins as weekend getaways, but most people packed their gear and headed to the mountains for the ever-expanding variety of recreational activities that included ice skating, boating, water skiing, hiking, horseback riding, golf and swimming, hunting and tobogganing.

The biggest and most active mountain town was Lake Arrowhead, where community activity centered around the charming Tyrolean village built in the early '20s. "Sportland" at Lake Arrowhead Village offered bowling, billiards, an arcade and a rifle range. New interest in skiing called for lifts and the development of more groomed slopes. Mt. Baldy was the favorite local winter ski resort, and in 1952, three "modern" twin-chair ski lifts were installed providing access to thirteen miles of ski slopes. Mt. Baldy's "Notch" Café at the 7800-foot-level Sugar Pine ski lift claimed to be "one of the world's most picturesque restaurants and the perfect place to warm up and eat after a day on the slopes."

Boys' and girls' summer camps and family dude ranches were at the peak of their popularity in the '50s. The Glenn Ranch Camp, located in the foothills of the San Bernardino mountains above Fontana near Lytle Creek, was promoted in a 1958 brochure as "Southern California's finest youth camp and the

local trees were sugar-coated in bright colors and artistically detailed inside and out. Mature pines and giant striped and polka-dotted cement mushrooms provided the landscaping. Employees costumed as elves, gnomes and pixies sold tickets and souvenirs, operated the rides and served food and refreshments. Santa Claus, Mrs. Claus, the Easter Bunny and Jack-the-Pumpkinhead greeted guests. There was a twenty-passenger Candy Cane Sleigh pulled by live arctic reindeer named Dancer, Prancer, Donder and Blitzen, a spinning Christmas tree where guests rode in the ornaments, burro rides and a miniature train ride "through the enchanted forest." Other attractions included a petting zoo, the Chapel of the Little Shepherd, Wee Marionette Puppet Theater, Santa's House (where kids could check to see if their names were in the "good book"), a "help yourself" lollipop tree and the North Pole, where the ice never melted, no matter how hot the Southern California sun was in the summertime.

scene of many an exciting historical chapter of bloody shootings, Indian raids, cattle rustlers and Gold Rush millions."

But it was the arrival of Santa Claus and his contingent, in 1955, that brought even more crowds to the mountains. Santa's Village, opened near Lake Arrowhead, was a fifteen-acre, larger-than-life toyland designed to keep the legend of Santa Claus and the spirit of Christmas alive throughout the year. Open every day but Christmas, admission was twenty-five cents for children and fifty cents for adults. Cartoon-like rustic buildings made from logs cut from

**LAKE ARROWHEAD VILLAGE LINEN POSTCARD, 1950.** Built in the Tyrolean mode of the old-world in the early '20s, Lake Arrowhead Village was the center of activity in the quaint mountain community. There were shops, restaurants, a market and an arcade. The North Shore Tavern, "the all-year mile-high resort hotel," had an expansive private beach and heated pool overlooking the lake. Rooms and cabins were offered with tile baths and showers: $8.50 a night for singles, $18 for suites.

**IDYLLWILD INN, 1959.** Set among towering pines high in the mountains, the Idyllwild Inn was typical of Southern California's rustic style mountain resorts. It offered steam-heated rooms and cabins, coffee shop, restaurant, the "Pine Room" cocktail lounge and a complete range of summer and winter activities.

Mt. Baldy brochure, 1953. Mt. Baldy became Southern California's favorite ski resort in the 1950s. The social scene included après-ski nightclubs with music and dancing. The "Alpiners" played in the Alpine Room at Vernon's Mt. Baldy Lodge. The Ice House Canyon Resort was advertised as "the liveliest nightspot in the Southland," and "not even the famed La Cienega Blvd. restaurant row can compare to the unsurpassed cuisine." The European Rathskeller served special "skier dinners" while polkas played on the jukebox.

Big Bear Trout Club, Big Bear Lake, 1959. The colorful orange and turquoise décor is a striking contrast to the three classic paintings on the wall.

Resorts & Campsites

Summer Camp, Big Bear, 1957

Greetings from *Santa's Village* California

Santa's Village Welcome House, 1959.
"Where you'll walk back into your own
childhood and lose your heart!"

Santa's Village

**SANTA AND THE "NORTH POLE,"
SANTA'S VILLAGE, 1955.**
The main attraction and the center-piece of Santa's Village, the "North Pole" was a pole of ice that never melted.

**SANTA'S VILLAGE,
SKYFOREST, 1955.** The towering candy cane signpost outside the main entrance was the most popular posing spot at Santa's Village.

**TOY SHOP, SANTA'S VILLAGE,
1955.** Elves in the Mill Wheel toy shop sold robots and model cars, boats, buses, trucks, tractors, trains and toy soldiers. Santa's Doll House was filled with hundreds of dolls imported from all over the world.

# Chapter 9

# BY THE SEA

Marineland, Pacific Ocean Park, the Nu-Pike. Beach volleyball, surfing, skin-diving. A giant roadside Santa Claus. Lawrence Welk and his Champagne Music Makers. These were the sights and sounds of Southern California beaches in the

ARAGON BALLROOM, LICK PIER, SANTA MONICA, 1951. While on the road with his Champagne Music Makers in 1951, maestro Lawrence Welk stopped in Santa Monica to visit the old Aragon Ballroom on the Lick Pier where he had played a few years earlier. The ballroom was suffering hard times so Welk offered to skip his next out-of-town engagement and play there for the next four weeks. As luck would have it, local television station KTLA had cameras in place at the ballroom for another show and decided to begin broadcasting *The Lawrence Welk Show* live every Friday night. Television audiences loved the show and it became a huge local success. In 1955, the show went nationwide on ABC. In 1958 the Aragon Ballroom became part of Pacific Ocean Park. Lawrence Welk and his crew were the amusement park's star attraction, performing to capacity crowds on Friday and Saturday nights.

1950s. Seaside cities and resort towns were bustling with sun worshipers, sportsmen and thrill seekers.

The Pike, the old-fashioned, Coney Island-style, beachfront amusement park in Long Beach, famous for its old wooden roller coaster, was refurbished in 1950 and renamed the Nu-Pike. At about the same time, the Dolphin Club of Compton won the first national skin diving competition at Laguna Beach. In 1951, the popularity of the new sport led to the first magazine for skin divers and spear fishermen, *The Skin Diver*, which began publication in Lynwood. Each issue featured diving news from the Seals of Santa Barbara, Los Angeles Neptunes and other local diving clubs, and pictured a bathing beauty dubbed "Miss Driftwood," modeling the latest in flippers and diving masks. The Spearfisherman Shop in Huntington Beach began manufacturing underwater frogsuits, which were advertised as "one piece, seamless pure gum rubber with nude freedom."

Beach volleyball was also an extremely popular local sport. When the first tournament was

held in Santa Monica in 1948, the winners each won a case of Pepsi Cola. By the early '50s, summer tournaments were being held in Santa Barbara, Corona Del Mar, Laguna Beach and San Diego and each included a "Queen of the Beach" beauty contest. Little did the pioneers realize that beach volleyball would become an Olympic sport.

Lawrence Welk and his troupe of singers, dancers and musicians began drawing crowds at their regular performances in the old Aragon Ballroom on Lick Pier in Santa Monica. Within a few months, KTLA began broadcasting the shows live every Friday night. When he died in 1992, Welk owned large amounts of real estate in Santa Monica.

In 1954, the "world's largest oceanarium," Marineland, opened in Palos Verdes, not far from the Wayfarer's Chapel, an architectural wonder that had been constructed a couple of years before, designed by Frank Lloyd Wright's son Lloyd. *Sea Hunt,* the television series which ran from 1957 to 1961 starring Lloyd Bridges as an undersea investigator, filmed most of the underwater scenes in Marineland's giant fish-filled tanks. In 1958, the historic Ocean Park Pier in Santa Monica was redeveloped and became spectacular Pacific Ocean Park, a nautically themed amusement park created to compete with Disneyland. And that year when the Four Preps sang "Twenty-six miles across the sea, Santa Catalina is a-waitin' for me," a trip to Catalina Island was an exciting adventure aboard an amphibious seaplane, a Catalina Airlines DC-3 or the *S.S. Catalina,* "The Great White Steamer."

By the late '50s, the underbelly of Southern California's beach culture was beginning to attract attention. The alternative free-spirited lifestyle of the local beatniks and surfers who were rejecting middle America's work-hard-and-live-happily-ever-after-in-the-suburbs ethic were on the verge of creating Southern California's cultural revolution. In the mid-'50s, beatniks began settling in Venice. They were an eclectic intellectual group of pre-hippie types who were attracted to Venice because of its historic character, cheap rent and tolerant populace. Many of the new residents were artists, writers and musicians. They often

hung out in coffeehouses such as the Gas House and Venice West Café, where they listened to poetry readings, jazz combos and folk singing.

At that same time, the general attitude toward surfers as beach bums and dropouts from society changed dramatically. In 1959, when the population of hard-core surfers in Southern California numbered fewer than a thousand, *Gidget,* the first mainstream movie about surfing, was released. The movie sparked a new surfing craze that attracted masses of Southern California teenagers to the ancient Hawaiian sport. The younger generation glamorized surfing for the first time and gave it an upbeat, youthful and clean-cut image. That soon led to local multi-million dollar surfboard, surf art, surf fashions, surf music and beach-movie industries.

BATHING BEAUTIES, PACIFIC PALISADES, 1951. A bevy of babes pose at a women's club "bathing suit revue" at the home of the aquatic silent movie star and one-piece bathing suit pioneer Annette Kellerman.

"THE SURFER," WOOD BLOCK BY SURF ART PIONEER JOHN SEVERSON OF SAN CLEMENTE, 1958. In 1960, Severson founded *Surfer Magazine.*

hundred dollars. Towering over the highway and calling, "Welcome to Santa Claus!" through a loudspeaker, the giant Santa became an instant landmark. Mrs. McKeon opened a shop where she sold date shakes, seashells and Christmas ornaments. As tourist trade increased, the McKeons expanded with a series of "Santa" shops; Santa's Toyland, Santa's Date and Olive Shop, Santa's Trading Post, Santa's Pottery Shop and Santa's Western and Novelty Shop. A playground was added with swings and a small merry-go-round. A forty-passenger miniature replica of a Southern Pacific Streamliner circled the shops. Santa's Kitchen served Vixen Burgers in the Reindeer Room, which was decorated with Christmas trees year-round. On the restaurant's roof there was a twenty-foot Frosty the Snowman. Santa's sleigh and team of reindeer were strung on cables flying away into the sky. In 1957, a post office substation was established in the date shop where mail could be postmarked "Santa Claus, California."

SANTA CLAUS LANE, HIGHWAY 101, 1954. Overlooking the ocean just south of Santa Barbara, Santa Claus Lane opened in 1948 as a juice stand. In search of a theme to attract passing motorists, the owner, Patrick McKeon, named it "Santa Claus, California" in honor of California's other "Santa" cities. During the 1950 Christmas season, while McKeon was dressed as Santa waving cars in from off the highway, a man stopped and offered to build a Santa Claus on top of the juice stand for five

*Santa Claus Lane*

**MUSCLE BEACH, SANTA MONICA, 1957.** Muscle Beach was ground-zero for Southern California's legendary fitness craze. It began in the 1930s when a group of men started doing gymnastics on the beach in Santa Monica. By the 1950s the open-air temple of the body beautiful was a famous showplace of scantily clad men, woman and children showing off their physical strength, agility, balance and fitness in a wide variety of solo, duo and group displays and activities. There were barbells, rings, uneven bars and platforms for those who wished to really demonstrate their physical prowess. On the weekends as many as ten thousand spectators would crowd the boardwalk to watch the incredible demonstrations. The human pyramid was always a crowd favorite. Hollywood talent scouts discovered a rich supply of beefcake and cheesecake and, more importantly, stunt men and women.

**HOT DOG ON A STICK, MUSCLE BEACH, 1956.** Originally called Party Puff, Hot Dog on a Stick started at Muscle Beach in 1946. The corn bread batter was "grandma's recipe."

**NU-PIKE BOARDWALK, LONG BEACH, 1953.** An old-fashioned waterfront carnival a la Coney Island existed right in downtown Long Beach. Conveniently located at the end of the Red Car line, the Pike began just after the turn of the century as "The Walk of a Thousand Lights," a boardwalk for a fashionable hotel and plunge. By World War II, the Pike had become fifteen colorful acres of thrill rides, freak shows, penny arcades, shooting galleries, shows, bars and tattoo parlors catering to a less-than-wholesome Red Car-riding beach crowd and the thousands of sailors stationed in Long Beach. Movie theaters, bingo palaces, dance halls, a plunge, bumper cars, a merry-go-round, a double Ferris wheel, coin-operated fortune tellers and the Tunnel of Love were all emblazoned

**THE CYCLONE RACER, NU-PIKE, 1950.** Billed as "the greatest ride on the face of the earth," the roller coaster was a Long Beach landmark and the Pike's most thrilling attraction. Built in 1930, the legendary ninety-six-foot-high all-wooden coaster had two side-by-side tracks. The forty-second ride began with the cars starting together then racing all the way to the finish. On the last dip, the cars dropped ninety feet at a fifty-degree angle at eighty miles an hour. The screams could be heard a block away. Over the years the rickety roller coaster claimed the lives of more than a few drunken sailors who ignored the sign that read "Do Not Stand Up."

with neon signs. In 1950, freak shows included a tattooed man, a bearded lady, a sword swallower, the "wild man" and the "dead man." The "wild man" was a guy yelling and screaming in a metal pit and swinging a metal chain against the walls and floor. The "dead man" was Elmer McCurdy, a bank robber who was killed at the turn of the century, then mummified. He was displayed at many carnivals around the U.S. before ending up at the Pike in the '40s.

"THE NU-PIKE, LONG BEACH," WATERCOLOR BY NEIL JACOBE, 1950. In 1950, the City of Long Beach attempted to change the seedy image of the Pike and make it more family-friendly by dressing it up with a fresh coat of paint, towering decorative light fixtures and by changing the name to the Nu-Pike. But it was too late, and the Pike's reputation couldn't be changed.

The Nu-Pike

**Marineland of the Pacific, 1954.** Luxuriously located on ninety acres of choice bluff at the tip of the Palos Verdes Peninsula, Marineland was a major Southern California attraction. Catalina Island was the focal point of the picture-perfect 180-degree ocean view. There was an adjoining ten-room motel and circular gift shop. Penguins and flamingos greeted guests at the main entrance.

**The Porpoise Room Cocktail Lounge, Marineland, 1955.** Decorated with seashells, coral, starfish and seaweed patterned carpet, Marineland Restaurant was divided into three connecting circular glass rooms, two for the dining room and one for this cocktail lounge.

Visit Southern California's
# MARINELAND
on the Pacific Ocean between
Redondo Beach and San Pedro
near Los Angeles

world's most spectacular
## CIRCUS of MARINE LIFE

**Fish Tank, Marineland, 1954.** The monumental ultra-modern structure contained two enormous side-by-side tanks with more than four thousand fish and other sea creatures including sharks, turtles, stingrays, barracudas, eels, octopi and a four-hundred-pound bass named Bertha. Several times a day a diver dressed in classic *Sea Hunt*-style scuba gear hand-fed the fish while visitors watched through three levels of underwater picture windows. Performing seals and walruses had their own arena and a three-thousand-seat theater where they played games and did balancing acts. Special holding tanks held sick and injured marine life rescued from the wild, while specialists nursed them back to health and returned them to their natural habitats.

**Bubbles, Marineland, 1957.** A pilot whale named Bubbles was added to the marine menagerie and became the big star of the show. Marineland claimed that it was the only whale in the world in captivity.

SUMMER 1953

ENJOY
THE WORLD FAMOUS SIGHTS
OF BEAUTIFUL

CATALINA

TIME TABLE · FARES
GENERAL INFORMATION

*Catalina Island, brochure, 1953.*

*S.S. Catalina, docked at Avalon, 1957.* Known as "The Great White Steamer," the *S.S. Catalina* was built and began service to the island in 1924. During the 1950s, one round-trip was made daily departing from Wilmington at ten in the morning and returning at four-thirty in the afternoon. As the ship arrived in Catalina, a sleek wooden "Miss Catalina" speedboat raced around the ship and boys would dive for coins tossed from the ship. Many of the ship's passengers arrived at the *S.S. Catalina* dock in Wilmington on the Pacific Electric Red Car's "Special Catalina Steamer Train" until the line was discontinued in 1958. The *S.S. Catalina* was retired in 1975.

*Catalina Airlines DC-3, Long Beach Airport, 1958.*
After World War II, when Catalina's "Airport in the Sky" reopened, United Airlines offered DC-3 service to Catalina from Burbank, Los Angeles and Long Beach airports. Following United Airlines' operation, Catalina Airlines was formed and operated twelve-passenger "De Haviland Doves" and thirty-two-passenger DC-3 service until 1959. In 1953, Avalon Air Transport, Inc. began seaplane service to Catalina from Long Beach and San Pedro. The fleet included nine-passenger "Grumman Goose" amphibious planes and forty-six-passenger Sikorsky flying boats. The trip took twenty minutes and the planes landed and took off in the bay at Avalon.

*"Catalina Cappy-the-clown," aboard the S.S. Catalina, 1959.*

*Avalon, Catalina Island, 1955.* By 1958, Catalina Island had been a popular tourist and resort destination for almost fifty years. Longtime attractions included the flying fish, the glass-bottom boat view of the undersea gardens, the exotic bird park and the live big-band music broadcasts and dancing at the famous island's famous casino. In 1950, a modern marvel, the Submarine Diving Bell was Catalina's newest attraction. It was a small undersea-viewing capsule that submerged two passengers thirty-five feet below the ocean's surface.

Catalina Island

Neptune's Courtyard main entrance, Pacific Ocean Park, 1959. The spectacular space-age starfish structure over the ticket booths was the icon of Pacific Ocean Park. It was set on a platform over pools with waterfalls, fountains and sculptures and decorated with a towering trio of sea horses and translucent aqua and clear plastic bubbles.

PACIFIC OCEAN PARK, SANTA MONICA, 1958. In 1956, The Los Angeles Turf Club and CBS acquired the lease on twenty-eight acres of Santa Monica beachfront property and the historic Ocean Park Pier. They proposed to transform and expand the weathered and out-of-date beachfront amusement area into a spectacular ten-million-dollar nautical-themed amusement park to compete with Disneyland. Hollywood's top designers and special effects experts were hired. The pier's vintage roller coaster, merry-go-round, fun house and several other classic attractions were redressed and included in the new park. General admission was ninety cents. Corporate sponsors shared the expenses and attached their logos to some of the new rides. The first attraction through the gate was Neptune's Kingdom, an underwater diorama presented by Coca-Cola. Motorized artificial turtles, manta rays, sawfish and sharks swam in place next to hundreds of fish hanging from strings. The Westinghouse Enchanted Forest was a trip into the future. The exhibit included the latest Westinghouse appliances in a model home that was part of a futuristic atomic city model. The robot recycled from the Westinghouse exhibit at the 1939 New York World's Fair and the world's first nuclear submarine, complete with its Westinghouse atomic engine, were also part of the exhibit. A Union 76 logo towered over Ocean Highway, an Autopia-like ride where drivers steered miniature cars out over the water and back to the edge of the pier. The Ocean Skyway transported passengers in glass bubbles seventy-five feet above the ocean to the end of the pier and back. Clowns, dolphins, sea lions and a live elephant covered completely in pink make-up performed together in the Sea Circus. 'Round the World in 80 Turns had tub-like cars sharply turning back and forth to show travel scenes from around the world. Passenger complaints of nausea and neck pains forced officials to close the ride after the first year. On Mystery Island at the seaward end of the pier across a rickety suspension bridge above a giant waterfall, the Banana Train ride was an adventure through a tropical jungle storm, past a bubbling volcano and a simulated earthquake. The park also had numerous traditional carnival rides disguised with ocean-themed motifs and names like Mr. Octopus, Mrs. Squid and Flying Fish. There were games and shooting galleries, a kiddyland called Fun Forest and live animals in Zooland. In 1967, after struggling to compete with its competitors, parking problems and weathering from the salt air, Pacific Ocean Park closed.

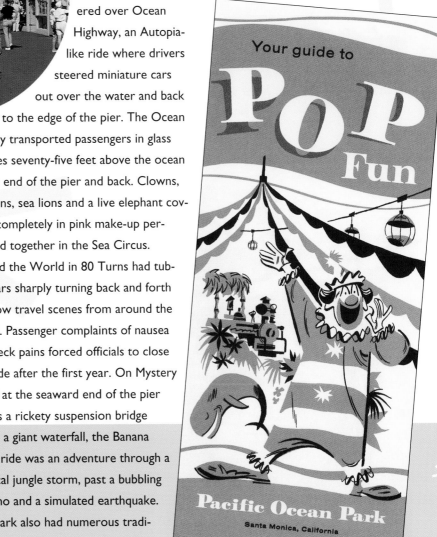

Your guide to

POP Fun

Pacific Ocean Park
Santa Monica, California

Flight to Mars entrance, Pacific Ocean Park, 1958. Inside, passengers sat in a spaceship and were 'transported' to Mars.

The Neptune sculpture pool at Pacific Ocean Park's main entrance, 1958.

Pacific Ocean Park

# Chapter 10

# FAIRS, FESTIVALS, PAGEANTS AND PARADES

Beauty queens, fruits, flowers, history, art, the catch of the day—just about anything was cause for Southern Californians to celebrate in the '50s. Chiefly sponsored by the Chambers of Commerce or local fraternal organizations, the annual fairs,

with western dancing, parades and a costume ball, and the Ramona Pageant, "California's Greatest Outdoor Play," was staged in a natural outdoor amphitheater in Hemet. In May of 1958, Jimmy Durante and Jayne Mansfield attended Garden Grove's first Strawberry Festival. Also in May, Lakewood's Pan American Festival honored countries south of the border and Joshua Tree held its annual turtle races. In June, the Flying Fish Festival drew crowds to Catalina Island and Beaumont honored its favorite fruit with a Cherry Festival.

July was the busiest month for Southern California celebrations. The world's longest picnic table was the center of the annual July 4th All-States Picnic in Ontario. More than one hundred thousand people gathered at the mile-long table that was divided alphabetically into sections for each state to reminisce with kinfolk from their home states. The festivities included an ant mascot, free fresh-squeezed Sunkist orange juice and a parade of beauty

festivals, pageants and parades, whether large or small, began as homespun promotions that inspired community spirit, gathered crowds, created publicity and promoted business.

Every weekend of the year, somewhere in Southern California there was a spectacle to see. During the first three months of the year Mother Nature was on parade. The first and most famous event was the world's most elaborate floral display, Pasadena's Tournament of Roses Parade. Following it, in February, camellia festivals were held in San Diego, Temple City and at Descanso Gardens in

La Cañada. That same month, the Riverside County Fair and Date Festival honored the rich harvest from the date palms of Indio, and the Fiesta of Hot Waters in Desert Hot Springs celebrated the bubbling wells of that resort community. In March, the Sierra Madre Wisteria Festival celebrated the blossoms on the world's biggest wisteria vine, the Swallows Day Parade welcomed the legendary return of the swallows to San Juan Capistrano and the National Orange Show, was held in San Bernardino.

In April, the Palm Springs Desert Circus Parade was a week-long event queens from every state. Meanwhile, in Newport Beach, the wealthy dressed down and had a "Tramp Steamer" Character Boat Parade. And at Venice Beach, the Surfestival showcased swimming races, a bathing beauty contest and men's physique competition. The Arts Festival and Pageant of the Masters was held in Laguna Beach. In Long Beach, beauty contestants from all over the world competed in the first Miss Universe Pageant in 1952. In August, the Japanese Nisei Festival was held in Los Angeles, the Corn Festival in La Habra and fiestas in Santa Barbara and San Diego recalled California's rich Spanish heritage. In September, the prettiest, most freckled, youngest, oldest and most talented twins were prized at the Twins Convention in Huntington Beach. The Fisherman's Fiesta celebrated the yearly catch in San Pedro while over a

million visitors went to the Los Angeles County Fair in Pomona.

In October, champion yarn-spinners gathered around a campfire to compete for the title of the tallest storyteller in the Peg Leg Liars Contest in Borrego Springs and a children's Halloween Costume Parade was held in Anaheim. The Long Beach All-Western Band Review was held in November, just before Los Angeles hosted the Great Western Livestock show. The biggest month of the year for elaborate pomp and circumstance was December. During the Christmas season Santa made an appearances in every town. His most celebrated arrival, however, was on Hollywood Boulevard at the Santa Claus Lane Parade.

As television became more popular, many of the events were featured on local stations. Queens who were crowned and trophies, blue ribbons and gold medals decorating the best of the best were good subjects for local news teams. The 1952 Tournament of Roses Parade made it to national television and by 1954, it was broadcast in living color. And by then, the whole country knew that the sun shone in Southern California on New Year's Day and the flowers bloomed in abundance. In the eyes of the rest of the United States, Southern California had something to celebrate.

**NATIONAL ORANGE SHOW, SAN BERNARDINO, 1951.** "America's Most Beautiful Agricultural Exposition," the National Orange Show, has been a tradition in San Bernardino since 1911. Throughout the '50s many California cities and counties showcased their citrus harvests with elaborate exhibits made of oranges and lemons. In 1958, Sunkist and the National Gas Bureau cosponsored the Gas Oven Derby, "the world's largest baking contest." Contestants baked orange cakes and lemon pies in 110 new automatic gas stoves.

**CAMELLIA FESTIVAL CHILDREN'S PARADE, TEMPLE CITY, 1956.** A tradition since 1945, the highlight of the Camellia festival was the parade of children and the young king and queen. The youngest queen, crowned in 1950, was eight months old.

**BEAUMONT CHERRY FESTIVAL, 1951.** The little fruit inspired the first festival in 1918.

1952
PASADENA
THEME
"DREAMS OF THE FUTURE"

Tournament of Roses souvenir postcard foldout cover, 1952.

Tournament of Roses

The Tournament of Roses Parade, Pasadena, 1954.

A New Year's day tradition in Pasadena since 1890, the Rose Parade began with the town's elite decorating their horses and buggies with flowers to parade down Colorado Boulevard on their way to the park. The press spread the word nationally about Southern California's beautiful New Year's Day weather and the abundance of beautiful blossoms.

LOS ANGELES COUNTY FAIR GIANT MIDWAY, POMONA, 1959. By the 1950s, this garden, barnyard and pop culture showcase had long been the largest county fair in the United States. From its start in 1922, countless contests, displays, demonstrations, exhibits, shows and parades revealed and rewarded the "amazing achievements" of each passing year. The elephant trams (there were four of them), came from the 1939 San Francisco Golden Gate International Exposition. In 1948 they were purchased by the Los Angeles County Fair.

THE FAIR'S FAIREST, L.A. COUNTY FAIR, 1955. Beauty queens pose for judges and photographers.

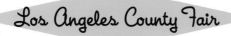

*Los Angeles County Fair*

PORKY, L.A. COUNTY FAIR MASCOT, 1948. In the mid-'50s, the creators of the famous cartoon character, Porky the Pig, claimed the rights to the name. That resulted in a "change-the- name contest" at the fair. The winning name, Thummer, was inspired by the wooden cutouts of the pig placed at nearby intersections hitchhiking to— and pointing in—the direction of the fairgrounds.

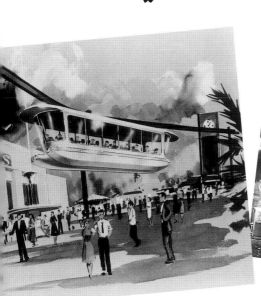

THE FUN ZONE, L.A. COUNTY FAIR, 1950. Spanning the entrance to the fair's amusement area, this spectacular sign was built in 1950.

**FLAGS EXCHANGE CEREMONY, PAN AMERICAN DAY, LAKEWOOD, 1956.** Started in 1948 by Lakewood Lions Club members, a former Bolivian Consul and his neighbor, Pan American Day honored a different Latin American nation each year, and consuls general from many different Latin American countries rode in a parade on the final day.

**RAMONA PAGEANT BOOKLET, HEMET, 1958.** A tradition since 1923, by the 1950s the Ramona Pageant was the oldest continuing drama in the United States. Presented in the Ramona Bowl, a natural amphitheater in the hills above Hemet, the play is generously staged on the slopes of Mt. San Jacinto with a cast of more than 350. The pageant was inspired by Helen Hunt Jackson's 1884 novel, *Ramona,* after the author became involved in Southern California's Indian Rights movement. Though Jackson was trying to improve the treatment of the native Californians, her book was a big success—just not in a way Jackson had intended. Her message of reform was ignored. Instead *Ramona* took on a life of its own, and Jackson's glorious portrayal of life in Southern California and its beautiful landscape turned the region into a popular tourist attraction.

**"OLD SPANISH DAYS," SANTA BARBARA, 1950.** Santa Barbara's "Old Spanish Days" Fiesta was one of several festivals held annually in various Southern California communities during the '50s which honored California's Spanish heritage with shows, parades, dances and fireworks. In San Diego, a similar celebration was called the Fiesta Del Pacifico. The festivities there included a national baton twirling contest and the "California Story," a ballet-pageant-musical set on seven stages with a cast of more than 1300 actors singers and dancers.

**GEISHA GIRLS PARADE IN LITTLE TOKYO AT THE JAPANESE NISEI FESTIVAL, 1956.** A Little Tokyo tradition since 1934, the week-long festivities included tea ceremonies, a judo tournament, *ondo* dancing, a baby show, Japanese floral arranging and a kimono-clad queen.

RAMONA

*Presented by the People of Hemet and San Jacinto*

THE CENTENNIAL PRESENTATION OF "OLD SPANISH DAYS IN SANTA BARBARA"

Fiesta

AUG. 23, 24, 25, 26, 1950

**DATE FESTIVAL BUILDINGS, INDIO, 1957.** Inspired by the Coachella Valley's annual date harvest, the Riverside County Fair and Date Festival started in Indio in 1921. In honor of the date's Middle Eastern origins, the fair adopted an Arabian theme in 1947. The next year, a permanent stage was built for the fair's nightly performance of the Arabian Nights Pageant, "a magic fantasy of the desert east with brilliant music, drama and dance." The set was a recreation of an authentic marketplace in "old Baghdad" designed by a Hollywood set decorator.

**RIVERSIDE COUNTY FAIR AND DATE FESTIVAL SOUVENIR PROGRAM, 1957.** Among the hundreds of exhibits in 1957 was the Atomic Energy Commission's Atoms for Peace exhibit. The Date Festival's most unusual events, the ostrich and camel races, are still traditions.

Date Festival

Queen Scherazade, Indio, 1955. The Date Festival queen and her court parade in a 1955 Cadillac Eldorado Biarritz.

Miss Universe, Long Beach, 1959. The newly crowned Miss Universe of 1959 takes a victory ride in a Chevrolet Impala convertible through downtown Long Beach. Her prizes included a fox stole, a set of Samsonite luggage and a one year contract with Universal-International Studios. The Miss Universe Beauty Pageant began in Long Beach in 1952. It was co-sponsored by Catalina Swimwear, Pan American World Airways and Universal-International Studios in Hollywood. Young ladies were invited to enter by sending photos of themselves wearing new Catalina swimsuits. The festivities included a parade of the beauties modeling Catalina's "official Miss Universe" swimsuit while posing on individual floats each hand-pulled by a sailor. For the first three years of the pageant, the official beauty consultant and makeup artist was Barbara Blakeley, who later became Mrs. Frank Sinatra. In 1960, the pageant moved to Miami Beach.

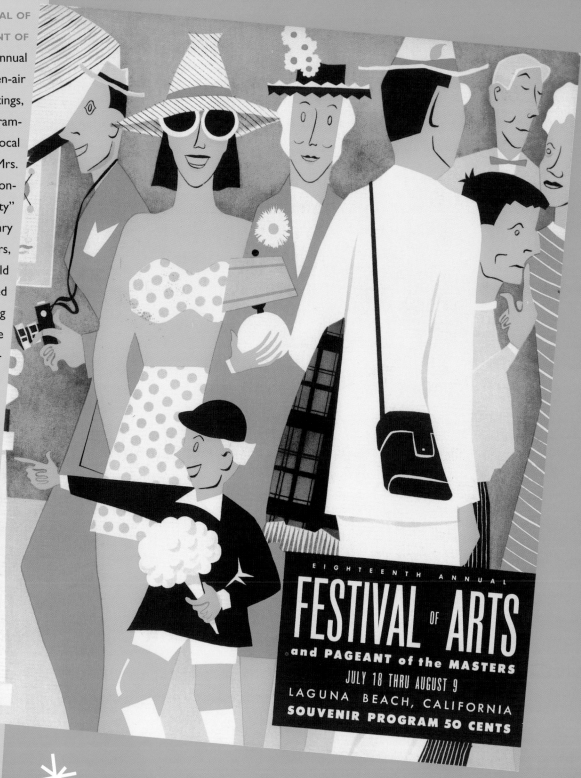

**LAGUNA BEACH FESTIVAL OF THE ARTS AND PAGEANT OF THE MASTERS, 1953.** An annual event since 1935, this open-air gallery showcases the paintings, sculpture, photography, ceramics and crafts made by local artists. In the 1950s, Mrs. Edward G. Robinson sponsored the "art of celebrity" gallery with works by Henry Fonda, Ginger Rogers, Claudette Colbert, Harold Lloyd, Harpo Marx and Fred MacMurray. Each evening during the festival, the Pageant of the Masters presented live models posing in ambitious life-sized recreations of famous paintings and sculptures. In 1953, the pageant included a special tribute to the fifty thousand Boy Scouts holding their third annual Boy Scouts Jamboree in Newport Beach, then concluded with the show's traditional finale, *The Last Supper*.

EIGHTEENTH ANNUAL

**FESTIVAL** OF **ARTS**

and PAGEANT of the MASTERS

JULY 18 THRU AUGUST 9

LAGUNA BEACH, CALIFORNIA

SOUVENIR PROGRAM 50 CENTS

Tramp Steamer Character Boat Parade, Newport Beach, 1958. The "SS Poopalong–1st Class Only" was just one of the crazy "Tramp Steamers" cruising at cocktail hour in this annual event. The fun was inspired by the whim of Disney animators Dick Shaw and Virgil Partch, who started the tradition in 1955 with members of the Newport Beach Punting and Sculling Club.

Boat Parades

**SAN PEDRO FISHERMEN'S FIESTA, 1957.** "A Whale of a Tale" was just one of the two hundred decorated boats parading in the 1957 Fiesta. Following an Old World custom, each September San Pedro's deep-sea fishermen celebrated their annual catch of a half billion pounds of fish. They secretly decorated their boats in secluded coves and hideouts, then revealed them for the thirty-five-mile parade around Los Angeles Harbor. The two-day festivities included a fish feast, knot-tying and rope-splicing contests and the blessing of the fleet.

Hollywood Santa Claus Lane Parade, 1955. Seen from the Broadway department store at Hollywood and Vine, the Santa Claus Lane Parade was the biggest and most star-studded of the countless Christmas parades in Southern California during the 1950s. It was started in 1928 to lure Christmas shoppers away from downtown Los Angeles to the newer stores in Hollywood.

# Chapter 11

# GLAMOUR LAND

Hollywood was promoted as the most glamorous place on earth in the 1950s, and few people argued the point. Marilyn Monroe, Elvis, Marlon Brando, James Dean, Doris Day, Audrey Hepburn and Elizabeth Taylor were well on their ways to

exotic organist sporting a jeweled turban, were among local television's first stars. By 1950, sixteen percent of Southern California

becoming legendary stars. The Sunset Strip, Coconut Grove, Hollywood and Vine, Grauman's Chinese Theatre, Schwab's and the original Brown Derby were world famous landmarks. Nightlife was dressy, with furs and tuxedos de rigueur. Romanoff's, Perino's and Chasen's were the sites of the most fashionable dinners. The Beverly Hills Hotel, Beverly Wilshire and new Beverly Hilton Hotel were the in spots for out-of-towners. Gilmore Island was the home to the Farmers Market, the Pan Pacific Auditorium, the Hollywood Stars baseball team at Gilmore Field and CBS

Television City. In 1954, the premiere of the film *A Star is Born* starring Judy Garland, at the Pantages Theatre, was the most star studded in Hollywood history.

But, after more than a generation of classic movies and stars, the phenomenal success of television was the talk of the town. *The Hollywood Reporter* proclaimed "TELEVISION IS HERE!" in January of 1947, when Bob Hope announced the premiere broadcast of KTLA, the first commercial television station west of the Mississippi. In 1949, KTLA began pioneering on-the-spot news coverage. And in 1958, KTLA unveiled the revolutionary "Telecoptor," and sent the first live television pictures from the sky directly into living rooms throughout Southern California. Wrestling champ Gorgeous George, western star Hopalong Cassidy, Bozo the Clown and Korla Pandit, an

households had television sets and Los Angeles led the nation with seven local television stations. Along with the big ABC, NBC and CBS network shows, Los Angeles's local stations entertained their rapidly growing audiences with a wide variety of programs that were broadcast live. Serials, dramas, westerns, musical shows, game shows, grand openings, sporting events, old movies and a host of characters—including animals—all became part of the daily lineup.

In 1950, Desi Arnaz and Lucille Ball formed Desilu to produce their comedy show, *I Love Lucy.* They invested $12,500 and rented a sound stage at the Motion Picture Center in Hollywood. Within six years Desilu was a fifteen-million-dollar-a-year business, producing eleven programs a week. As the television industry snowballed, Hollywood's sound stages—from Burbank to Culver City—were jammed with new productions. Many old movie sets and costumes were recycled and used for television productions. Employment for entertainers, actors, writers, musicians, producers, directors and technicians was booming. Many actors who had a hard time making it big in the movies found success in the new medium. The new television studios could barely keep up with the gargantuan appetite of the new living room audience. CBS built the world's first studio designed exclusively for video production in 1952 and dubbed it Television City. The corporate catch-phrase announced on the air before every presentation originating from the new state-of-the-art facility was "From Television City in Hollywood . . . ."

By this time, the movie studios were putting out more hours of film for television than they were for motion pictures, since many former moviegoers were happy to stay home and be entertained by their television sets. Movie studios responded by investing millions in elaborate, innovative and technically complicated "bigger and better than ever" 3-D and wide-screen formats with names such as Cinerama, Cinemascope and Vista-Vision, in hopes of luring their once-faithful audiences back into theaters.

By 1959, Hollywood Boulevard had a less-than-glamorous-anything-goes reputation and the glitz of Las Vegas had eclipsed the glamour of the Sunset Strip. The Mocambo and Ciro's, the last nightclubs from Hollywood's heyday, had closed. Twentieth Century-Fox announced major plans to demolish one hundred eighty acres of old backlot movie sets and develop the site as Century City, a town-within-a-town that would eventually become a commercial center.

But Hollywood was determined not to lose its aura as the world's most glamorous place. With a conciliatory attitude, the local leaders of Hollywood established the Walk of Fame, the area's first revitalization project that paved sidewalks with 1,558 stars commemorating the biggest names in films, television and music. The "entertainment industry" now referred to all the fields of glamour that Hollywood could call its own.

CAPITOL RECORDS, HOLLYWOOD, 1957. Built in 1956, the world's first round office building quickly became Hollywood's most futuristic icon. Its below-ground recording studios were the first ever built for high fidelity recordings. The light on the tip of the spire continually blinks H-O-L-L-Y-W-O-O-D in Morse Code.

PERSIAN ROOM, BEVERLY HILLS HOTEL, 1956. High fashion flair was the order of the day in pink, black and white.

PAN PACIFIC AUDITORIUM, LOS ANGELES, 1952. Built in 1934, the spectacular streamline moderne façade made the Pan Pacific one of Los Angeles's most famous architectural landmarks. Throughout the 1950s, it remained a premier indoor special events center. It was used for Ice Capades shows, custom car shows, General Motors Motoramas, home shows, sportsmen shows, circuses, conventions, political rallies, concerts, hockey, tennis and basketball games. In October of 1957, Elvis performed at the Pan Pacific in his gold lamé suit before a crowd numbering nine thousand.

Looking north, Sunset and Vine, Hollywood, 1952. Beginning in the late '30s Sunset and Vine became the hub of Hollywood with NBC, CBS and ABC radio studios, theaters and restaurants located just steps from each other. In 1952, CBS expanded its facilities with Television City and in 1955, NBC built "Color City," in Burbank.

MODEL OF CBS TELEVISION CITY ON DISPLAY AT FARMERS MARKET, 1951. With cane and hat in hand, Earl B. Gilmore, president of the Gilmore Oil Company inspects the plan for the huge studio compex to be built on the property adjacent to Farmers Market. Completed in 1952, at the cost of seven million dollars, Television City was ultra-modern in shape, style and function.

GILMORE FIELD, LOS ANGELES, 1950. Constructed in 1938, "Friendly Gilmore Stadium" was home to the Hollywood Stars, a Pacific Coast League baseball team owned by Bing Crosby, Barbara Stanwyck and Cecil B. DeMille. When the Brooklyn Dodgers moved to L.A. in 1957, the Stars were transferred to Salt Lake City and the stadium was torn down in 1958.

Farmers Market, 1958. Opened in 1934, Farmers Market had blossomed into a "must see" tourist attraction and Los Angeles's most unique marketplace by the '50s. The one hundred fifty individually owned open-air fruit-and-vegetable stalls, cafés, gourmet shops, specialty shops and services, and an international bazaar called the Foreign Patio had a reputation for selling the very best. Everything from Shrimp Louis to mynah birds to steamship tickets to grass skirts was available.

FARMERS MARKET FRUIT AND PRODUCE

LEE AND ANNA PYATT

TOWN AND COUNTRY VILLAGE, LOS ANGELES, 1959. Located directly across the street from, and similar to, Farmers Market, Town and Country Village was promoted as having a more continental atmosphere and more sophisticated shops than its neighbor.

FARMERS MARKET

The Coconut Grove, Los Angeles, early '50s. Opened in 1921, the Coconut Grove was the showplace of the Ambassador Hotel, home to famous big bands and big name entertainers. By the '50s, it was one of Los Angeles's most enduring dining and dancing supper clubs and remained popular among the Hollywood nightclub crowd. Dominated by tropical palms, the room was detailed with a Moroccan motif, gold leaf, etched-palm-tree doors and stuffed monkeys. In 1957, the room was redone in red and the palm trees were thinned out and rearranged. For Judy Garland's two-week engagement in 1958, opening night was black-tie only.

The original Brown Derby, Wilshire Boulevard, Los Angeles, 1950. Opened in 1926, by the '50s, the Brown Derby was one of the most famous relics of the early days of Hollywood. There were three other Brown Derby Restaurants (Los Feliz, Beverly Hills and Hollywood and Vine) but only the original on Wilshire Boulevard was shaped like a hat.

Brown Derby, Hollywood and Vine, 1950. Entertainer *Jimmy Durante* lunched with friends below his caricature at the second Derby.

**MOCAMBO CLUB, SUNSET STRIP, 1950.** The popular jazz ensemble, the Firehouse 5 + 2, made up of Disney animators, promoted their regular Monday night Mocambo performances and Charleston contest with a sidewalk performance on the Sunset Strip. The Mocambo was one of Hollywood's most fashionable nightclubs. Inside, an aviary of parakeets, macaws and cockatoos were the finishing touch to the stylish décor.

*Romanoff's, Rodeo Drive, Beverly Hills, 1956.* Begun in 1941 and at this location since 1951, Romanoff's was known for serving the finest French cuisine in town and was one of *the* places to see and be seen. Humphrey Bogart, Louis B. Mayer, Clark Gable, Frank Sinatra, Lana Turner, Groucho Marx, Cole Porter and Alfred Hitchcock were all regulars. The colorful owner, Michael Romanoff posed as a snooty descendant of the Czar of Russia complete with a fake accent. He occasionally sported a turban and regularly dined alone in the restaurant with his two pet bulldogs seated at his table. Although it was home to the original Rat Pack, the ultra-conservative Romanoff began handing out right-wing literature along with the menus and the restaurant's popularity began to decline. Romanoff's closed in 1962.

*KING AND I* PREMIÈRE, GRAUMAN'S CHINESE THEATRE, 1956. Built in 1927, the Chinese Theatre had long been Hollywood's most popular tourist attraction. The most photographed and famous forecourt movie-star-footprint ceremony was in 1954, when Marilyn Monroe and Jane Russell performed the ritual to publicize *Gentlemen Prefer Blondes*.

Out on the Town

# Chapter 12

# E TICKET

If ever there were a perfect time and place to create an entirely new concept of family entertainment, it was Southern California in the 1950s. On July 17, 1955, Walt Disney, the master of fantasy, dedicated Disneyland Park "to the ideals, the dreams and the hard facts that have created America . . . with the hope that it will be a source of joy and inspiration to all the world." And it was.

Disneyland was the first amusement park of its kind in the world. Environments defined by themes featured rides, exhibits, shows, music, architecture, transportation, animals, landscaping, food service, merchandise and costumed employees, all carefully planned to create a theatrical entertainment experience. The park was inspired from the famed animator's heart and made from scratch by hand with love and integrity. Walt Disney wanted the public to forget the outside world once they were inside his park. He wanted them to feel like they were in another world. His magical world.

Disney's dream to create a park that both parents and children could enjoy together began long before that grand opening day. According to Lillian Disney, Walt's wife, it was his lifelong fascination with trains that ultimately led to the creation of Disneyland. In 1948, when Walt attended the Chicago Railroad Fair, an exhibition celebrating one hundred years of railroad progress, he also visited Henry Ford's Greenfield Village, in Dearborn, Michigan. There the combination of the historic homes and buildings arranged in a town square setting with a main street and railroad station, an

antique carousel, stern-wheeled paddle-boat circling a small man-made island and vintage locomotive traveling around the property, had a profound effect on Disney's imagination. Less than a month after returning from the trip, Disney issued a heavily detailed memo outlining his ideas for Mickey Mouse Park, to be built across the street from the Disney Studio on sixteen acres in Burbank. Over the next four years Disney experimented with concepts and ideas for the park and changed its name to Disneyland. He recruited the most inventive and resourceful artists, designers and engineers—many from his own studio staff—to begin the most creative project ever imagined.

The first public announcement of the plan was the March 27, 1952 headline of the *Burbank Daily News*, "Walt Disney Make-Believe Land Project Planned Here." The scale of the plans outgrew the proposed site before Burbank city officials had a chance to deny Disney's request to build the park there. In August 1953, after many rural Southern California locations were secretly considered, all fingers pointed to a 160-acre orange grove conveniently located adjacent to the site of the proposed Santa Ana Freeway in Anaheim, a rural agricultural town. Just after the *Anaheim Bulletin* broke the news on May 1, 1953, that a location had been selected, Disney

struck a deal with ABC to produce a weekly television series for the network in return for help financing the park and thirty-five percent ownership. When the *Disneyland* show made its debut in the fall of 1954, Walt told his new TV audience of his plan to build "the happiest place on earth." The show featured live and animated segments that represented each of the themed lands together with weekly "progress reports" showcasing Disneyland Park's actual construction.

For the monumental task of supervising the construction of Disneyland, Walt hired retired Navy Admiral Joe Fowler, known to those close to him as "Admiral Can-do." Fowler had built ships in China before World War II and ran San Francisco's extraordinarily busy Navy Yard during the war. When construction began in July 1954, many of the workers—not accustomed to building a world of fantasy—required constant supervision. While the construction of Main Street U.S.A., Adventureland, Frontierland and Fantasyland progressed at a breakneck pace, Tomorrowland hadn't even been started. Time and money were running out, but Walt insisted that his "Magic Kingdom" wouldn't be complete without a world of the future. With less than six months before opening day left, work began on the "world of 1987."

Each land presented different obstacles but they were minor compared to creating the Adventureland Jungle Cruise, a lush tropical jungle complete with native huts, ancient ruins and a slew of alligators, monkeys, hippos and elephants. Originally Disney's plan called for real animals, but he soon realized that wild animals in a children's wonderland wasn't a practical idea. So he called upon his studio special effects team who had just created a remarkably realistic mechanical squid for the movie *20,000 Leagues Under the Sea*. They developed a cast of expensive mechanical animals, but that left little money in the budget for mature plants to create a realistic jungle. Bill Evans, the resourceful landscape designer, then took advantage of an fortunate opportunity presented by California's Department of Transportation. The state offered to take any of the trees that were in the paths of the rapidly expanding freeway system and transplant them to Disneyland.

During the frantic final days of construction and installation Walt lived in the park. After just 257 working days and seventeen million dollars spent, he and celebrity co-hosts, including Ronald Reagan, emceed a grand opening celebration with special VIP tickets for the press and celebrities. The festivities were televised live nationwide from twenty-two remote cameras placed throughout the park. Not all of the attractions were finished and there were some minor

glitches. But people, invited and uninvited, showed up to see the promised land in droves. There were counterfeit tickets, party crashers and fence climbers. The next day, ABC claimed it was "the biggest live telecast in history," and the general public was admitted for the first time. Admission was one dollar for adults and fifty cents for children. Attractions ranged from ten to thirty-five cents each. Less than two months after opening day, Disneyland Park welcomed its millionth guest. While the park's kinks were worked out, Walt turned his attention to expanding the park's potential. During the first twelve months the number of attractions more than doubled. As Walt Disney stated, "As long as there is imagination in the world, Disneyland will never be finished."

**GUESTS BOARD A DISNEYLAND STAGE LINES STAGECOACH, FRONTIERLAND, 1955. The stage coach rides were discontinued in 1960 after tipping over one too many times.**

*Sleeping Beauty Castle, the entrance to Fantasyland, 1955.* The center-piece and icon of Disneyland Park was named in anticipation of, and to promote, the Disney animated classic, *Sleeping Beauty*, which was released in 1959. Architecturally, the castle was inspired by the medieval Neuschwanstein Castle in Germany. Like most of the other buildings in Disneyland, forced perspective was used to make it appear taller than it actually is.

## Fantasyland

*Mad Tea Party, Fantasyland, 1955.* After visitors walked through Sleeping Beauty Castle, they found the original attractions including the Mad Tea Party, Dumbo Flying Elephants, King Arthur's Carousel, the Casey Jr. Circus Train, Peter Pan's Flight, Mr. Toad's Wild Ride and Snow White's Adventures. Originally Dumbo's big ears were designed to flap as they flew, but the ears proved to be too heavy and they kept burning out their little motors. King Arthur's Carousel was one of the few antique attractions in the park that was recycled from another location. Built in 1875 in Philadelphia, it was discovered and purchased for Disneyland in 1954 in Toronto, Canada. The hand-carved carriages and sleighs, horses and other animals were removed and restored. But when Walt specified that he wanted it to be a true carousel, which meant it would have only horses, more antique carousel hoses were purchased. The carriages, sleighs and other animals not used on the carousel were models for the cars of the Casey Jr. Circus Train.

**GUESTS POSE IN FRONTIERLAND WITH THE MARK TWAIN RIVERBOAT IN THE BACKGROUND, 1958.**
Among the original attractions in Frontierland were rides aboard stagecoaches, Conestoga wagons and pack mules on the winding dirt trails through the old west. The Indian Village represented the culture, customs and arts of Native American tribes, with teepees, totem poles, "join in" ceremonial dances and a chance to meet a full-blooded Indian Chief. The Golden Horseshoe Revue, a colorful live 1880s dance hall show, would ultimately find its way into the *Guinness Book of World Records* as the longest-running stage show in history. The most popular attraction was a picturesque journey down Rivers of America in Frontierland aboard the Mark Twain, the first paddle-wheeler built in the United States in more than fifty years. In 1956 Tom Sawyer Island was opened. During the first few seasons on the island there was a fishing platform where guests could fish. The fish they caught were cleaned and wrapped in plastic to go.

### Frontierland

**DUTCH BOY PAINT "COLOR GALLERY" BROCHURE, 1956.**
Because time and money were running short before the opening of Disneyland, Walt had to accept several glorified corporate "county fair" style exhibits to fill the buildings in Tomorrowland. They included the Dutch Boy Color Gallery ("Allow Paints to show you our future in colors"), the Kaiser "Hall of Aluminum Fame," Crane's "Bathroom of Tomorrow," and Richfield Oil's "The World Beneath Us," a "fast-paced animated history of man's quest for energy." In the American Dairy Association "Dairy Bar" exhibit guests could learn about future dairy activities including milk being delivered to a home by a milkman with a helicopter strapped to his back.

**TOMORROWLAND ENTRANCE, 1955.** The buildings closest to the entrance housed Circarama, a film tour of the western United States presented on a screen that totally surrounded the audience and The Monsanto Hall of Chemistry exhibit, "To demonstrate the contribution of chemistry to contemporary life . . . and the promise it holds for the future." The centerpiece, the giant "Clock of the World," told the time everywhere on earth. Shown in the distance, the TWA Moonliner, marked the entrance to the "Rocket to the Moon" attraction. The most popular original attraction in Tomorrowland was Autopia, "the freeway of the future." Other original attractions included Space Station X-1, "Circle the Earth from fifty miles up in this Satellite View of America," a walk through sets from the Disney classic *20,000 Leagues Under the Sea* and the Flight Circle where demonstrations were given of remote gasoline-powered model planes, cars and boats. The Astro Jets and Skyway opened in 1956. Disneyland Park's most valuable souvenirs were sold at the Tomorrowland Art Corner: original Disney animation cells for a $1 and full-size attraction posters for $1.35.

**MONSANTO'S HOUSE OF THE FUTURE, TOMORROWLAND, 1958.** Opened in June 1957, the House of the Future was a walk-through all-plastic showcase of the domestic style and technology of tomorrow. Perched atop a center support column, the four symmetrical wings "hovering" eight feet off the ground housed three bedrooms, two baths, a living room, dining room, family room and an "Atoms for Living" kitchen completely furnished with the finest modern designer furniture and accessories of the day. It showcased such innovations as speakerphones, electric toothbrushes, microwave cooking, disappearing appliances, atomic food preservation and big screen television. When Tomorrowland was remodeled in 1967, the House of the Future was demolished. According to an eyewitness, the wrecking ball just bounced off of the plastic walls, so it had to be cut apart.

Phantom Boats, Tomorrowland, 1955. Plagued with mechanical problems from opening day, the Phantom Boats were the first "permanent" attraction ever removed from Disneyland. Originally there were fourteen of the stylish big-finned fiberglass boats painted black, pink and turquoise. They cruised around the Tomorrowland Lagoon sputtering, overheating and stalling until they sailed into the sunset in the fall of 1956.

Tomorrowland